More Praise for *Socially ADDept*, Revised Edition

"*Socially ADDept* is a welcome and needed resource for parents of children with ADHD and/or Learning Disabilities. It is very painful to watch your child struggle in the social arena and not know how to help. This book provides parents with clear, practical guidance and step-by-step assistance... The information in this wonderful, reader-friendly book... (is) beneficial for parents trying to help their children develop and become more competent."

—**Sandra Rief, M.A.**, bestselling author of *How to Reach & Teach Children with ADD/ADHD, 2nd Edition* and *The Dyslexia Checklist*

Praise for the First Edition

"*Socially ADDept* provides information to de-mystify the behaviors of children with attentional problems. But beyond this, Dr. Giler provides specific strategies to deal effectively with specific social situations. Eminently readable, this book belongs on your bookshelf... but will undoubtedly not spend much time there. It is a book that will be used and referred to often!"

—**Richard Dr. Lavoie**, bestselling author of *It's So Much Work to Be Your Friend* and *The Motivation Breakthrough*

"Where do you turn when you find out your child has special learning requirements? It can be confusing, overwhelming and frustrating. *Socially ADDept* is the best learning tool a parent can use to help their child. It is clear, practical, easy-to-read and fun for kids and parents to use together. Dr. Giler has created the next best tool to having her in your home as a guide and expert. A must for every family with learning challenges!"

—**Cherie Carter-Scott, Ph.D.**, author of *If Life is a Game, These Are the Rules*

"I'd like to suggest an excellent book that can be used by parents who are interested in trying to help their child with his or her peer relationships. It is called *Socially ADDept*. I think you will find that this is really helpful in your efforts to assist your child in getting along better with peers. Professionals will find that this book can be quite helpful to them as well, especially in working with parents to help their child."

—**David Rabiner, Ph.D.**, Duke University and author of *ADHD NEWS*

Jossey-Bass Teacher

Jossey-Bass Teacher provides educators with practical knowledge and tools to create a positive and lifelong impact on student learning. We offer classroom-tested and research-based teaching resources for a variety of grade levels and subject areas. Whether you are an aspiring, new, or veteran teacher, we want to help you make every teaching day your best.

From ready-to-use classroom activities to the latest teaching framework, our value-packed books provide insightful, practical, and comprehensive materials on the topics that matter most to K–12 teachers. We hope to become your trusted source for the best ideas from the most experienced and respected experts in the field.

Socially ADDept

Teaching Social Skills to Children with ADHD, LD, and Asperger's

Revised Edition

Janet Z. Giler

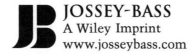

JOSSEY-BASS
A Wiley Imprint
www.josseybass.com

KH

Published by Jossey-Bass
A Wiley Imprint
989 Market Street, San Francisco, CA 94103-1741—www.josseybass.com

Jossey-Bass books and products are available through most bookstores. To contact Jossey-Bass directly call our Customer Care Department within the U.S. at 800-956-7739, outside the U.S. at 317-572-3986, or fax 317-572-4002.

Jossey-Bass also publishes its books in a variety of electronic formats. Some content that appears in print may not be available in electronic books.

Library of Congress Cataloging-in-Publication Data

Giler, Janet Z.
  Socially addept : teaching social skills to children with ADHD, LD, and Asperger's / by Janet Z. Giler.—Rev. ed.
      p. cm.
  Includes bibliographical references and index.
  ISBN 978-0-470-59683-8 (pbk.)
  ISBN 978-0-470-92592-8 (ebk.)
  ISBN 978-0-470-92593-5 (ebk.)
  ISBN 978-0-470-92594-2 (ebk.)
  1. Learning disabled children. 2. Behavior disorders in children. 3. Social skills in children. I. Title.
  LC4704.5G525 2010
  371.9′04482–dc22

                                        2010032220

Printed in the United States of America
REVISED EDITION
PB Printing 10 9 8 7 6 5 4 3 2 1

8/17/11

About This Book

Many children with Asperger's Syndrome, learning disabilities, Attention Deficit Hyperactivity Disorder, and other special needs misunderstand or don't know the "hidden" rules of communication. Many teachers and parents don't know what to do when children struggle with teasing or feelings of rejection. *Socially ADDept* makes this process easier for adults and children. Working with the ADDept approach, parents and teachers can help children

- Comprehend and use appropriate body language
- Handle teasing
- Increase their self-awareness
- Increase their respect for others
- Understand the rules of friendship
- Handle anger appropriately

This book is not a general, entry-level book on learning disabilities, Attention Deficit Hyperactivity Disorder, or Asperger's Syndrome. Diagnostic information is contained in the Appendixes, and there are many excellent introductory books on these subjects included in the Bibliography and Resources section.

Author's Note

Most of the lessons in Part Two can be done equally well by parents and teachers. The few that are more appropriate for parents to do at home with the child are marked clearly.

Also, a number of these exercises should not be done in front of an entire class as it could be embarrassing to a child if he makes a mistake in front of his or her peers. This includes all of the role play exercises and those in which adults are to give the child negative feedback. Alongside each of these exercises is a Note reminding readers to conduct these exercises in private with the child or in a smaller group setting in which the child is comfortable (with friends, trusted peers, or siblings).

About the Author

Janet Z. Giler, PhD, MFT, has been licensed as a family therapist since 1982. For the last twenty years, she has been offering training to parents, teachers, and mental health professionals about the particular needs of children and adults with ADHD, learning disabilities, and Asperger's Syndrome. Dr. Giler has spoken on national television and on radio and has appeared at numerous professional conferences on how to teach social skills to children with special needs. She is an approved supervisor with the American Association of Marriage and Family Therapists, and her articles have appeared in professional journals.

To contact Dr. Giler about private consultations, teacher training, or speaking engagements, please visit her Web site (www.addept.org) or e-mail her at jzgiler@cox.net.

Acknowledgments

I thank the following people for their time, support, help, and encouragement. Thanks go to my husband, Karl, for his patience, editorial support, and humor; my friends Julie Hanks, Sonja Lane, Diane Wolf, Ellen Biderman, Paula Meichtry, Dorothy Storer, Jane Yuguchi Gates, and Lori Cronyn for their comments. My acquisitions editor, Marjorie McAneny, should get an award for her persistence and guidance. Thanks are also due to Joan and Les Esposito of the Dyslexia Awareness and Resource Center for their support and encouragement, my son for allowing me to practice many of these techniques on him, and the children who attended my ADDept groups and taught me which techniques worked. I am also indebted to Henry Slucki, PhD, USC School of Medicine, who allowed me to intern in his laboratory where I learned the fundamentals of behavioral therapy.

Because children learn social skills from their peers, I also have to thank my anchor group of friends from junior and senior high school: Julie Krinberg Hanks, PhD; Ellen Geffner Biderman; Clara Greisman Mayer; Mauren Rosen Raynes; Marlene Kassel Josephs; and Shelley Surpin (who also did double duty as my attorney). I truly don't know where I would be if I had not had these women as a continuous source of support in my life.

Last, I would like to acknowledge two special people who were great teachers to me: my dear aunt, Dinah Mellon, PhD, and an old teacher, a man known in Cambridge as Karmu (Edgar Warner). Dinah taught me that no matter how good I thought I was at mind reading, "You always have to check to make sure you are right." I learned this concept when I was a teenager, long before I had even heard of the "theory of mind" concept (mind reading). Edgar Warner encouraged me to write. When I met him, I had undiagnosed dysgraphia, and when I told him I couldn't write, he just said, "That doesn't matter; you're going to do it anyway." This book is dedicated to both Dinah and Karmu.

Contents

Part II: The Socially ADDept Lessons

Contents   **xiii**

Contents   **xv**

Part III: Appendices

Introduction

All authors have a story about why they do what they do, and mine probably began with my having an undiagnosed learning disability. This disability was never labeled as such because I functioned above grade level. It wasn't until I got into college and failed the introductory English writing exam that I ever had to take any remedial classes. I was lucky because I was gifted in mathematics and abstract reasoning and managed to get through graduate school, though it took a lot of starting and stopping to finally get my PhD. I began focusing on learning disabilities as a problem or issue only when my son was diagnosed in kindergarten.

By the time my son was eight, I had learned a lot about learning disabilities and made it a focus of my doctoral studies. From watching Rick Lavoie's video, *Last One Picked, First One Picked On,* I knew my son needed to learn social skills. In 1993, there were not a lot of books or curricula for teaching social skills to children with learning disabilities or ADHD. I hired two therapists from Los Angeles, Karen Horowitz and James Kehr, PhD, who showed me their method of conducting social skills groups. After their training—and reading every curriculum I could find—I eventually wrote the ADDept Curriculum, a ten-week program for children who are in mainstream classes and are having trouble socially.

As I started to train therapists, I saw we needed a training video, so I produced *From Acting Out to Fitting In* (1998). One of the surprises that came from this experience was seeing that everyone associated with the project—the editor, the director, the cameraman, and the grip—all either had ADHD or learning disabilities themselves or knew someone who did. The film (now available on DVD) has helped many professionals learn how to run social skills groups. It has been gratifying to see that the ADDept program is now used in many school districts in the United States and abroad.

It seemed like a logical progression to write up the parent version of the ADDept Curriculum, and so with the help of Christine Nolt, *Socially ADDept: A Manual for Parents* was first published in 2000. It has been reprinted four times over the last ten years before being acquired by Jossey-Bass this year. This edition includes all the old material as well as new exercises that focus on children with Nonverbal Learning Disability as well as Asperger's Syndrome. Although the needs of each subgroup of children are quite different, the fundamentals of teaching social skills to children remain the same, despite their different disabilities.

Audience for This Book

Socially ADDept aims to help parents, teachers, and professionals teach children with special needs basic social skills. Although the book was primarily written for this audience, it can be used by anyone who wants to know how to teach social skills.

Although many teachers and parents know what to do with children who easily learn through imitation, many do not know how to help children who are struggling to learn. Many children need to cognitively understand all the parts of the process and need to have the skill explained in smaller, incremental steps. This book aims to provide a pragmatic approach to teaching social skills, by making the concepts simple and user-friendly.

> Although *Socially ADDept* was primarily written for parents and teachers, it can be used by anyone who wants to know how to teach social skills.

> For those who are not as interested in the theory behind *Socially ADDept*, you may wish skip to Chapter Two.

Theoretical Underpinnings

The theoretical underpinnings of this book come from my training in communication theory, social exchange theory, family systems theories, and Transactional Analysis. In social exchange theory, friendships are a commodity that is being constantly being traded and negotiated, with the bartering chips being positive or negative interactions (what Berne, 1964, called the *stroke economy*). People engage in this process of give and take by talking and listening, caring, sharing physical gifts, doing actions for each other, sharing physical affection, and so on. In all of these models, a common notion is that relationships are supposed to be reciprocal; however, they are often not equal, and when they are perceived as lopsided, the person who thinks he or she is receiving less often can become resentful.

Every friendship has certain costs and rewards. Many special needs (SN) children may require extra time and attention; therefore, it is important that they also learn what to do to give to the other person. By teaching them to pay attention to the other child's reactions, use empathy, say thoughtful words, and perform kind deeds, they show the other child that she is important to them. Likewise, it is important to teach them to remember to ask another child about people or events that are important to her. Instead of launching into their own issues or concerns, they need to spend more time paying attention or responding to the interests of others. Learning how to focus on the other child (person) helps restore balance in their relationships.

If these children are less skilled than their peers, they may have to work a little harder to keep friends. They may have to learn to be good listeners or to become more thoughtful. Because they often have inaccurate perceptions of their actions or their strengths and weaknesses, they will need to learn to see themselves more clearly. If they hurt someone, they need to learn how to apologize for what they did. Further, they have to learn how to solve conflicts without walking away from the friendship when they are hurt.

A seminal idea in this work is that internal thoughts and feelings rarely create problems between people. Although actions can create problems, by far the most common problem lies in how the other person's actions or words have been interpreted by the child with SN (who may, in fact, be misinterpreting the message). Instead of seeing an action as positive (and receiving a positive stroke), the child may view it as a criticism and react accordingly. The principle from Transactional Analysis (Berne, 1964) is that everything one says or does creates consequences or reactions in the other person. Berne viewed the exchange of positive and negative strokes as the fuel that ran the stroke economy (how he summed up the relationship between two people). The easy advice for children with SN is to give more than they take. Dinah Mellon, PhD (who, sadly, left no published works), a student of Dr. Berne, was an early constructivist who believed that every transaction either constructed or deconstructed the bond between people. The net exchange, if positive, brought people closer together. If negative, this exchange pushed them further away. In other words, whereas we can encourage children to think and feel whatever they like, they need to consider the consequences of what they say and do to another person; do they give more than they take? To use an analogy of a car's fuel tank, we want to encourage children to never let the gas tank become empty and always make sure they have something in the reserve tank. When people consistently takes more than they give, the other person feels depleted.

Another fundamental concept from communication theory (Bateson, 1972; Watzlawick, Breavin, & Jackson, 1967) is that every communication has two levels. The first is the explicit communication—the verbal, written, or digital communication; the second level contains the implicit message perceived through interpreting the nonverbal elements of the communication. This second level is called the meta-communication because it comments on the relationship between the people involved. People unconsciously understand the meta-message by mind reading the tone of voice, facial expressions, and gestures and then evaluating what they think it means. (People often have fights over "what he said," but they are often fighting over what they thought the person's meta-message meant.) Because the mind reading of the meta-message often occurs unconsciously, most people do not attempt to verify whether the meaning they have attributed to the meta-message is correct. The meta-message often supplies the context of the communication (the type of relationship) and certainly informs the listener of the emotional state of the person speaking.

The meta-communication is what gives children with SN so much trouble because it is unstated and requires mind-reading and checking abilities. Most of us don't pay conscious attention to this level unless we experience a discord

Mind Reading and Mind-Blindness

Mind reading and *theory of mind* are different names for the same concept. The terms refer to a person's ability to step outside his or her own frame of reference and project himself or herself into the mental state of another person to imagine what is in that other person's mind — what he or she is feeling, thinking, desiring, intending. Mind reading is how we understand others. This ability is present in very young children, who often can mind-read successfully by four or five years of age. *Mind-blindness* (not having the ability to mind-read) affects children (and adults) because they often react to a communication (whether verbal or nonverbal) without really knowing what the other person was feeling, thinking, desiring, or intending, which leads to many misunderstandings that often never get resolved (Howlin et al., 1999).

between the two levels, meaning that the words and the meta-communication don't go together. It is as though we are on autopilot until we hit a bump in the road; then the communication moves into our consciousness, and we ask questions or make comments to determine the meaning of the meta-communication. In other words, we check with the other person: "What did you mean by that tone [or that look]?" The problem for many children with SN is that they don't intuit the proper meaning; they often have poor mind-reading ability, referred to as *mind-blindness* (Howlin, Baron-Cohen, & Hadwin, 1999); and they fail to check (clarify) with the other, "What did you mean by that look?"

Many children with SN have trouble with any communication that isn't clear, and mind reading certainly can be ambiguous. To understand the communication, they need to understand the context, which relies on where the communication occurred and its ostensible purpose. Next they need to know something about the relationship of those who are involved in it. Much of this is perceived by reading body language. If children have poor mind-reading skills (mind-blindness), do not know the unstated rules of communication, and do not know how to read body language, they really are operating in the dark, and it is no wonder that they misperceive relationships and often react inappropriately to the situation. This book is dedicated to making explicit some of the more subtle pragmatics of social communication. I hope I have achieved my goal.

Part I

What Parents and Teachers Need to Know

Chapter 1

Why Children with Special Needs Struggle Socially

Many children with special needs make social mistakes. Although their problems differ vastly in scope, children with Attention Deficit Hyperactivity Disorder (ADHD), learning disabilities, and Asperger's Syndrome (AS) frequently have social problems because they do not understand nor use the same social conventions that others do.

Although their reasons for failing to use these rules or conventions are different, what is common is that many special needs (SN) children mishear words and misuse or misperceive the meaning of tone. They answer out of turn or fail to take turns, interrupt or change the subject, intrude into another person's space or activity, fail to respond appropriately to another's feelings (failure to use empathy), and, in some cases, fail to respond at all. By the age of five or six (and certainly by seven or eight), they are out of sync with their peers who have honed their mind-reading skills and can tell when someone disapproves of their actions and are able to modify their behavior to be more in line with what is expected.

Why Teach Social Skills?

Social skills enable children (and adults) to be successful in their social interactions. Whereas many schools know how to help children who struggle academically, less is known about how to help children who struggle socially. The assumption has been that children with SN will observe and copy their peers. We know now that this assumption is not correct. Many children with SN need specific instruction on how to implement social skills, and they need to receive feedback on how well they performed these skills. This is the piece that many social skills programs fail to include. Children need to learn how to read and respond to nonverbal communication, which they often overlook because of its ambiguity. As mentioned in the Introduction, the meta-communication level refers to the relationship between the participants and is comprehended mostly through mind-reading body language and tone. Children need to pay attention to this level, particularly when disapproval is being expressed, as this lets them know when to change their behavior.

Children with SN Often Make Social Mistakes Because They

- Mishear words
- Misuse or misperceive the meaning of tone
- Answer out of turn
- Fail to take turns
- Interrupt
- Change the subject
- Intrude into another's space or activity
- Fail to stop when asked

Why Children with SN Need Training in Social Skills

- Children with SN often don't know the rules of conversation.
- Many children with SN do not follow sequences. (Conversations are supposed to be sequential; you listen and then you respond. Many children with SN do not understand or follow this rule.)
- Children with SN often misinterpret or fail to interpret body language appropriately.
- Children with SN often violate the spatial boundaries of others.
- Children with SN often misperceive jokes or friendly teasing as hostility.
- Many children with SN have inaccurate awareness of self and other.
- There is no way to compensate for poor social skills.

Mind-Blindness

Children need to learn to identify when people disapprove of their actions so that they can make adjustments accordingly. When children have mind-blindness, they often have inaccurate perceptions of themselves as well as misperceptions of the role of the other person in a given dynamic. One of *Socially ADDept*'s first goals is to teach children greater self-awareness. The second step in gaining social awareness is for children to see how their behavior affects someone else. This skill involves stepping outside their own frame of reference to view an interchange the same way someone else might see it. (I refer to this as having *joint perception*; see Figure 1.2). This step involves a meta-communication, because both people need to comment about their verbal and nonverbal exchange by checking or verifying that what they saw and the meaning they attached to it are similar (or in some cases,

> The ability to mind-read disapproval verbally and nonverbally lets children know when to adjust (or correct) their behavior.

different). Finally, children have to learn to adjust their behavior to be more in line with what other people expect.

When Children Don't Stop

When children don't perceive that they are out of sync or fail to change their behavior, other children react by getting angry, frustrated, or hurt. If this discord persists, other children will ask them to stop. If the children continue to be annoying, the other children either avoid or chastise them. If children persist in being annoying or aggressive, in both cases ignoring what the other children want, the other children may label these children as self-centered or insensitive.

Language Difficulties and the Hidden Rules of Conversation

Social Problems Due to Language or Perceptual Sequencing Problems

- Failure to introduce a topic clearly
- Poor topic organization
- Faulty sequencing, such as jumping to conclusions without listening to the whole story
- Failure to respond to a topic
- Failure to share the conversation, often perseverating on a topic without paying attention to the interest of the other person

Many children with SN have problems with language. They may have difficulties with topic organization, or they may fail to introduce the subject. They may fail to see that conversations are supposed to be an exchange and hence perseverate on some detail, ignoring the bored body language that tells them to stop. They have missed the social rule that conversations are supposed to be an exchange between people. When a child engages in a lopsided conversation (more like a diatribe or lecture), the other children may make derogatory comments (which are intended to silence the offending child). Instead of understanding the message, the child with SN is often surprised. He may not understand that this is the way other children tell him to be quiet.

Tone is also often misused or misunderstood. Tone communicates the emotional state of the person speaking. Children are supposed to comprehend the emotional message that is being conveyed by the tone. Children may also be unaware of their own use of tone and how others may be reacting to the emotional message that their tone conveys. As an example, when children hear a monotone, they may react with discomfort or avoidance because it differs from what they expect.

Difficulty Recognizing and Labeling Feelings

Three Weaknesses That Make Decoding Feelings Difficult

1. Misreading or ignoring body language due to inability to read facial expressions or body gestures or posture
2. Missing the emotional meaning of tone through misinterpreting or ignoring the meaning of pitch (tone), volume, and intensity
3. Misperceiving or ignoring someone's personal space, failing to move when the person frowns to let you know that you are too close to him

Many children with SN have trouble accurately labeling their own feelings; likewise, they may misread or respond inappropriately to the feelings of others. If children fail to perceive and respond to what another child may be feeling, they appear to lack empathy (the ability to comprehend and respond to the feelings of others). Because this emotional message is more than half of the communication, ignoring it is considered a mistake. Misreading (or ignoring) another's feelings often leads to misunderstanding that person's intentions because the emotional message is supposed to be a cue as to whether or not the person is kidding, serious, angry, playful, and so on.

When children only rely on the literal meaning of words, they often do not understand joking and may feel that they are being teased. Because they may miss the friendly tone, they can misjudge the relationship and often miss the other child's intent. Because they may have difficulty distinguishing

Children expect their friends to demonstrate empathy (verbally or nonverbally). When children do not do this, they are often viewed as self-centered or callous.

hostile from friendly teasing, they often respond with protection and withdraw or respond with hostility.

Poor Problem-Solving Skills

The failure to comprehend other children's motivation correctly impairs children with SNs' ability to resolve conflicts. Instead of seeing a remark as an oversight, an accident, or a friendly jibe, these children may assume that the other child *intended* to hurt them. If they hold on to this negative perception, it is hard, if not impossible, to forgive the other child, to make amends, and to continue on with the friendship. Instead, friendships are ended prematurely. Instead of accepting apologies and maintaining friendships, many children walk away or retaliate when they have been wounded or hurt. They often do not bounce back or have other recuperation strategies. Others have noted that many children with SN ruminate on their negative experiences (Frankel, 1996; Frankel & Myatt, 2003). Ruminating on past negative events increases children's unhappiness and limits their adaptability (Brooks & Goldstein, 2002).

How Mind-Blindness Causes Conflicts

Mind-blindness causes problems when children

- Miss or misperceive the emotional message (body language and tone)
- Incorrectly predict the feelings, thoughts, and intentions of others
- Fail to check if their assumptions about the other person are correct
- Ignore or distrust peer relationships
- End friendships prematurely due to negative assumptions of the other child's intent ("He meant to hurt me")
- Escalate conflicts because they don't know how to communicate and accept differences and because they don't view the problems in the context of an existing relationship

As an example of how poor empathy and mind reading can spiral into a conflict that can threaten a relationship, consider Johnny, a seven-year-old child with Nonverbal Learning Disability (NLD). His friend Mike has teased him about telling silly jokes. Instead of remembering that Mike has been his friend in the past and is therefore probably kidding around, Johnny deduces that Mike is making fun of him and doesn't like him anymore. Johnny doesn't see the teasing in the context of their previous relationship history of being friends for the past year.

Instead of seeing that Mike may be (1) trying to tell him something or (2) just joking and playing around, Johnny gets offended. He doesn't correctly infer Mike's feelings or intentions (*Mike has been my friend, so if he tells me I'm being silly, it doesn't mean he doesn't like me anymore; it may mean that he's tired of hearing my silly jokes*). If he incorrectly labels Mike's intention as a put-down, he may feel hurt and overreact. Instead, he is supposed to take this as corrective feedback—in other words, a message that he should stop telling silly jokes.

This lack of resiliency deeply affects many children with SN. Instead of learning and adapting to new situations and acquiring new experiences and friends, many children with SN spend their energy struggling to make sense of their social environment and its changing requirements. Although some successfully learn the unwritten rules and acquire the skills of mind reading, empathy, and problem solving, others retreat or continue to use the same maladaptive strategies.

Failure to Mimic Behavior

Many children with SN aren't good at mimicking behavior. Because they may not perceive what the newest trends are, they often do not follow them. They may not pick up on the current fad, whether it is a knuckle bump or a phrase such as "Totally" instead of "Yeah, I know." Or they may show up in short shorts when long, baggy shorts are "in." They may greet another child with the same "Hello, how are you?" the first, second, and third time they see him or her at school, not realizing that the second time, they should modify the greeting to a "Hi" or a nod, and the third time, a nod. These are simple social rules that children with SN may not know to employ.

How Children Deal with "Different" Behavior

When confronted with behavior that is different from what is expected, most children will try to correct the offending child. Younger children are often more direct and will tell the offending child to stop. As children get older (third through sixth grades), their way of correcting another child becomes more indirect; they use gestures, exaggeration or sarcasm, corrective humor, friendly teasing, gossip, or avoidance to get through to the child who is breaking the tacit rules. However, if the child continues (to be aggressive, break the rules, interrupt play, or ignore the requests from other to stop), his peers will attempt to avoid him, often attributing negative characteristics, such as that he is "mean," "weird," or "odd." The child can become socially isolated and may acquire a bad reputation (which makes it more certain that he will not be invited to participate in new situations). In the best circumstances, children are ignored or neglected by their peers.[1] In the worst cases, the child is rejected, which can cause the labeled child to experience anxiety or depression. They may not know how to change his social predicament.[2] (Children with ADHD, particularly those who are aggressive, often break rules and can be disruptive or aggressive and can find themselves rejected for these behaviors.)

Why Train Preadolescent Children?

By third or fourth grade, when their peers are making "best friends" and are starting to set up their own socializing dates (and enjoying academic success), children with SN may be on the social periphery. Their social and psychological problems escalate as the children age. Undiagnosed adolescents are more likely

Socially ADDept

to drop out of high school; many join gangs or join others who use drugs and alcohol or engage in high-risk behaviors, such as unprotected sex, or even criminal activities.[3] Many of these problems could be avoided with early intervention. Children with SN from poorer communities are more likely to be overlooked or misdiagnosed because their problems are often attributed to other issues, such as poverty, lack of socialization, or personal problems stemming from abuse or neglect.

The years before puberty, the latency years, offer a unique window of opportunity to teach social skills that can have significant ramifications for children's self-esteem (Erikson, 1968). Erikson termed the developmental task of this stage as "industry (competency) versus inferiority;" if children do not develop a sense of competency at this stage, they are at greater risk for low self-esteem and even depression. Because all children are experimenting with identity during this stage, friendships and social ties are more flexible. This makes it an optimal time for children to learn new skills that they can use before and during their transition to junior high, where the friendship circles become less permeable and crowds and cliques are formed.

Two Major Weaknesses That Lead to Social Mistakes

Two Major Areas of Weakness

1. Breaking social rules or conventions
2. Deficiencies in interacting skills

As already discussed, children with SN frequently make mistakes in two major areas: (1) following social rules and conventions and (2) using good interacting skills. The first group of errors is related to the misuse of body language or the lack of comprehension of the other children's body language (kinesis); the misuse of pitch and tone or lack of comprehension of its meaning (vocalics); and the misunderstanding of the rules of personal body space, so that they may violate another's spatial boundaries (proxemics). As an example, using inappropriate humor may not be a serious mistake, but failing to stop when asked to do so is. Ignoring the command to "knock it off" (STOP) can lead to an aggressive interchange that can end a friendship.

Twelve Mistakes That Can Ruin Friendships

Breaking of Social Conventions or Rules

- Misusing and misinterpreting body language (kinesis)
- Misusing and misinterpreting tone (vocalics)

(continued)

(continued)

- Misusing space and violating another's space (proxemics)
- Intruding into activities or groups and being critical or aggressive when refused
- Ignoring commands to stop

Deficient Interacting Skills

- Failing to react to or understand the feelings of others
- Responding excessively to teasing
- Attributing negative intentions because the child uses black-and-white thinking and sees the other person as being "for me or against me" (D. Mellon, personal communication, 1960)
- Failing to use social memory
- Failing to respond with empathy
- Getting stuck emotionally (ruminating over events)
- Being unaware of how his or her behavior affects others

The second set of problems stems from failures to identify clearly and respond to the feelings of others. If children misinterpret or misperceive the intention of another child (thinking, for example, *He wants to hurt me*), they will react by either withdrawing or attacking. Many children do not compile and use their social memory (the ability to recall the events that have occurred within the relationship, which includes remembering significant events or conversations with their friends). Using social memory enables children to put the current incident in the context of their shared history. When children have a conflict and do not put it in context every problem, if not solved successfully, can threaten the relationship. For example, if children don't remember their friendship with another child, they are apt to misinterpret a wisecrack as an insult, often responding aggressively. If they had put the "misdeed" into a context (using their social memory), they might have avoided reacting with hostility.

Children (especially girls) need to be taught how to engage in "rapport talk," conversations that are primarily focused on the feelings of both participants (Tannen, 1992). Instead of sharing facts, the children share events, with particular attention paid to how they felt in response to the event or interchange. The listener's role is to acknowledge and respond (verbally and nonverbally) to the other person's feelings.

Girls use and expect others to engage in rapport talk. When girls do not respond to their friend's feelings or fail to remember an event that was important to her, the girl may feel disconnected. Because many children with SN have trouble remembering facts, much less what happened to someone else, it is important that children use such tools as friendship cards (see Exercise 6, Lesson One) to help increase their social memory.

Black-or-White Thinking

Many children with SN reduce complex emotions or thoughts to simpler categories, with the intention of aiding their comprehension. This reduction of feelings or intentions into simpler, contrasting categories has been termed *black-or-white thinking*. The child may see the other person as being *for me* or *against me,* or think *he likes me* or *he hates me.* Black-or-white thinking is rarely accurate, as most feelings and intentions are more complex and fall within the gray area. If children see the world in black-or-white terms, they will fail to understand that feelings can be ambiguous, contradictory, or neutral. Black-or-white thinking also gets in the way of correctly inferring what the other person may be feeling and lead to inaccurate predictions of the other's intention.

Teaching Children with SN the Behaviors of Popular Children

In a study of popular children, Fox and Weaver (1989) found that popular children engage in the following behaviors when confronted with social situations: (1) they smile and laugh with other children, (2) they greet other children by name, (3) they initiate conversation by asking questions and showing interest, (4) they extend invitations to others, (5) they give compliments, (6) they share, and (7) they pay attention to their appearance. They also have better problem-solving abilities, are able to mind-read, are more resilient when hurt, and use their social memory to ignore mild insults or friendly teasing. Most social skills training methods have focused on teaching children with SN to avoid annoying or problematic behaviors, but teaching children how and when to use positive behaviors is more effective.

Children also need to acquire more accurate self-perception and become more aware of how their behavior affects others. If children just learn the skills by rote and do not acquirer greater self-perception, they will most likely have trouble generalizing the skills into other situations or environments.

Social Behavior of Popular Children

1. Smile and laugh
2. Greet others by name
3. Initiate conversations, ask questions, and show interest
4. Extend invitations
5. Give compliments
6. Share
7. Have neat appearance

The Importance of Early Intervention

All children benefit from early intervention. The brain continues to grow and change throughout life (this is known as *neuroplasticity*). Most of the growth occurs through making new neuronal connections, which often occur while learning new activities or skills (adults with ADHD or learning disabilities have often remarked that they didn't feel as though they were totally "wired" until they were in their mid- to late twenties.)

Early interventions are best for all children but are particularly important for children who have Asperger's Syndrome and other forms of ASD (Autism Spectrum Disorder, see Appendix C). Although children with Asperger's Syndrome can learn well, they may choose to avoid interacting with others because they often do not know how to react. There is a popular misconception that children who have ASD will never speak. The findings of a longitudinal study showed that only 14 percent of autistic children were unable to talk by age nine, and 40 percent could speak fluently. However, the children who learned to speak before the age of five or six years had the best outcome (Lord, 2002).[4]

Teaching Joint Attention

New research in autism indicates that children with ASD benefit from training in *joint attention,* and when they have learned this skill, they develop more sophisticated language skills.[5] In Figure 1.1, the child and the adult both use joint attention. They both focus on the object, an apple, at the same time and check with each other to see if they both saw the same object (or the child attempts to share the object with the adult). Research shows that joint attention can be taught to infants as young as nine months (Mundy, Sigman, & Kasari, 1990; Mundy & Crowson, 1997; Whalen & Schreibman, 2003). This research concluded that children who learned joint attention increased their interactions by pointing to events or objects, showing toys, or looking at the other person while inspecting a new object. Children who use more joint attention also increased their language abilities. This is significant because children who do not develop language skills (talking before age five or six) are more likely to have trouble developing peer relationships.[6]

Two Major Deficits

Although many social problems are due to lack of skills, not all children who are having social problems need to learn new skills. Suppose, for example, that you ask a young girl who failed to listen, "Do you know how to listen?" If she responds by telling you exactly how she is supposed to do it, she mostly likely has a performance problem (Gresham & Elliott, 1994). Children with performance problems don't need to be retaught the mechanics of how to perform specific skills, as they already know how. Instead they need help in

Figure 1.1 Parent and Child Sharing Joint Attention

handling their impulses, which get in the way of performing what they know they should do. In contrast, children with acquisition deficiencies have not acquired the knowledge needed to perform the skills.

Two Categories of Children with Social Skills Problems

Children with Acquisition Deficits

- Don't know the mechanics of the appropriate behavior
- Don't see themselves accurately
- Can be withdrawn, anxious, or depressed

(continued)

(continued)

Children with Performance Deficits

- Know what they are doing wrong but have trouble controlling themselves
- Can be hyperactive or impulsive (ADHD)
- Can have problems controlling their anger

Performance Deficits

Children who have performance deficits fail to act on their knowledge because they have insufficient control of their emotions and impulses to regulate their behavior. Many children with ADHD can be in this category, as they all have trouble controlling their impulses (see Appendix A). Children who cannot control their behavior need interventions to enable them to increase their impulse control. Some children will need medication to control their impulsivity or aggressiveness (or both). Behavioral therapies that have shown results include behavior modification programs, cognitive therapy techniques for monitoring emotions and consequent behavior, charting, reprimands, time-out, and clear "if-then" consequences. Children with performance deficits benefit from behavioral management programs that include parental education. Once children are able to control their impulsivity, they can receive social skills training if they need it.

Therapies for Performance Problems

- Behavior modification programs
- Cognitive therapy
- Clear consequences as in "If you do _____, then _____ will happen."
- Charting
- Time-out
- Consistent reprimands and rewards
- Medication

Acquisition Deficits

Socially ADDept was designed to train children who have acquisition deficits. These children have not acquired the pragmatics of social skills, and when asked, they will tell you that they do not know how to perform the skill. They may also have trouble choosing which skill fits which situation. They often do not know why they should use the skill. Their processing deficits are often responsible for impeding their learning, and many children in this group have processing problems, the basis of all learning disabilities (see Appendix B.)[7]

These children may not see themselves accurately or may not be able to describe what they observe other children doing because they may not be able to break the skill down into its component parts. Many have poor mimicking skills or poor body perception. These children need to learn how (1) to use and recognize verbal and nonverbal emotional expression, (2) to understand the reasons why the skills need to be performed (for children with AS and NLD in particular), (3) to perform the skills (pragmatics), (4) to accurately assess how well they performed the skills (feedback), and (5) to use alternative behaviors. Children also have to learn to step outside their own frame of reference (perspective) to see if they share the same perception of an interaction that the other person has, which is referred to as *joint perception.*

In Figure 1.2, the teacher observes the boy fighting with another boy. The boy shares with the teacher that he is also aware that he fought with the other boy and that he was unhappy about it (see facial expression). The teacher and the boy jointly share the same perception of the interaction between the two boys.

Sharing joint perception is a meta-communication, as it not only involves reflecting on an interaction but also checking or verifying with someone who observed the interaction that one's verbal and nonverbal interpretation of what occurred is correct or incorrect (Mundy, Gwaltney, & Henderson, 2010). This example illustrates a meta-communication between the teacher and the boy. The boy describes what he thought occurred and the teacher describes what she saw. The child has to step outside his own perception as he compares his version of what occurred with the teacher's observation. They have joint perception when they both see the interaction the same way. This is an invaluable teaching tool, as children with SN often do not see how their behavior affected someone else. This step of checking and verifying requires both self-evaluation and confirmation from an outside observer.

Ten Essential Skills for Being Socially ADDept

Most curricula rely on teaching structured learning in which the children rehearse and practice their new skills with feedback. *Socially ADDept* differs from other programs in its emphasis on rating the child's self-perception. (The children earn extra points when they have accurate joint perception.) When children improve their self-evaluation skills (use better self-evaluation and joint perception), they become more resilient (Brooks & Goldstein, 2002). Because interactions are fluid and can easily be altered by changing the tone,

Figure 1.2   Teacher and Student Share Joint Perception

the words, or the body language, it is important that children learn how (and when) to change their behavior so that they can alter the outcome of a given interaction.

Socially ADDept was designed to address the most common social errors made by children with SN. The lessons are intended to be sequential, but there is obvious overlap. Most children with social problems have trouble accurately reading and using appropriate body language. They often use tone inappropriately. Many get too close too quickly and violate others' physical boundaries (personal space). Many perseverate (defined as talking at length about a topic without any regard to the interest of the other person). Many children fail to show interest in others by failing to ask questions or stay on topic. Others do not use social memory and show no concern for events that are important to their friends. But by far the most significant problem is failing to mind-read disapproval so as to adjust their behavior. Because mind reading is fundamental to understanding and correctly inferring the intentions of others, children with SN often overreact or react inappropriately to teasing, often getting angry and failing to apologize when they have wronged someone else. Last, they often fail to see interactions from the other person's point of view. In essence, they often are out of sync with accepted social rules and conventions (etiquette).

Socially ADDept breaks these skills into ten lessons that are taught as sequential building blocks:

1. Understanding friendship: What are friends? How do we make friends? Why are listening and responding important? What do friends share? (Exercises for this lesson are about building positive self-esteem, setting goals, and identifying personal interests.)

2. Being a good listener

3. Using conversational skills—listening, greeting others, asking questions, giving compliments, sharing the airtime—and understanding the four levels of friendship

4. Understanding the importance of body language—facial expressions, gestures, personal space, appropriate touching

5. Understanding tone and the feelings that tone communicates; learning how to be in sync using the same pitch, volume, and tempo

6. Recognizing friendly behavior; understanding what it means when the words and the body language disagree

7. Joining a group or an ongoing activity; understanding special issues for girls; dealing with refusal and scouting out social opportunities

8. Dealing with teasing, recognizing the three forms of teasing, and understanding how boys use status humor

9. Managing anger; dealing with outbursts and employing damage control; knowing how and when to apologize

10. Understanding cell phone etiquette and the rules of cyberspace; understanding cyber-bullying and when to get adults involved

Socially ADDept Goals

- To develop the child's self-awareness
- To recognize and respond to the feelings of others
- To accurately read nonverbal signals to infer the other's intention
- To solve problems instead of ending relationships

(continued)

(continued)

- To increase self-awareness
- To increase mind-reading ability
- To increase the child's ability to engage in joint perception of social interactions
- To have and use recuperation strategies

Notes

1. Cowen, Pederson, Babigan, Izzo, and Trost (1973) classified children as rejected, neglected, withdrawn, controversial, and popular. Rejected children were found to have more significant life adjustment issues: rejected boys were inappropriately aggressive, disruptive, and frequently broke rules; rejected girls were also more physically aggressive than their peers. The researchers concluded that being rejected seemed to correlate with significant life adjustment issues.

2. Unfortunately, negative reputations have an impact on how successful children will be socially. Once established, a poor reputation appears to be fairly stable over time. Frankel (1996) and Laugeson and Frankel (2010) discuss how to change a bad reputation in an exercise included in the curriculum at UCLA's Parenting and Friendship Program.

3. Research figures vary, but it is clear that students with ADHD (and some with LD) drop out of high school more frequently than those without this diagnosis and are more likely to get into trouble with the law. There is a strong correlation with substance abuse (Curran & Fitzgerald, 1999). Bierman and Wargo (1995) found that adults with ADHD constituted 9.1 percent of the prison population (in a random sample). Other studies have suggested a higher percentage. (It is still twice the prevalence of ADHD in the general population, which is estimated to be between 3 and 5 percent (Bierman & Wargo, 1995; Mannuzza, Klein, Konig, & Giampino, 1989).

   The Santa Clara County Juvenile Justice system's model program for the coordination of diagnosis and treatment of children with SN is called "Project YEA!" (see their Web site www.sccgov.org). The program estimates that 30 percent of incarcerated youth need special education and states that if all children were tested, another 20 percent would qualify for services. The program's publication *Special Education Rights: Bench Guide* was drafted and finalized by Judge Richard Loftus and was distributed statewide. It covers special education law and its application in juvenile court.

4. The University of Michigan is conducting an ongoing longitudinal study of children with ASD. Similar to the findings of Kasari at UCLA, the

Michigan study (Lord, 2002) showed that children who received simple training in speech skills prior to age two were more likely to talk by age five. Lord has developed a screening tool to detect autism that is widely used. Information on the study is available from the University of Michigan's Autism and Communications Disorders Center's Web site: http://www.umaccweb.com/research/studies.html.

5. There are many researchers doing complementary work on ASD and Asperger's Syndrome, specifically training children in joint attention. The research is occurring at many universities throughout the United States and internationally. See, for example, Kasari, Paperella, Freeman, and Jahromi (2008); Mundy et al. (2010); Mundy et al. (1990); Mundy and Crowson (1997); and Koegel and Koegel (2009).

6. Koegel and Koegel (2009) found that four methods are very effective in remediating some issues in children with ASD: Applied Behavioral Analysis (ABA), Discrete Trial Training (DDT), Pivotal Response Training (PRT), and LEAP (Learning Experiences: Alternative Program for Preschoolers and Parents). Their research shows that parents' participation is a crucial element in all training programs, as parents spend more time with their children than anyone else. For example, when parents are trained to encourage joint attention, as they are in PRT, their children had significant language gains. (PRT has been done with infants as young as nine months old.)

7. Maedgen (2000) found that among the various subtypes of ADHD, the inattentive and combined types of ADHD responded well to direct instruction in social skills. This may not be surprising, as it is estimated that nearly 50 percent of children who have ADHD, inattentive form, also have learning disabilities.

Chapter 2

Tips for Communicating with Children

To teach children to be *Socially ADDept* is a team effort. Ideally, everyone in the child's environment would be recruited to help the child learn social skills. Although this isn't a realistic expectation, it is possible for parents, teachers, and other personnel who work with these children (including a group leader if that option is available) to agree on how they approach them both in terms of the targeted behaviors that they wish to reinforce and the manner in which they give feedback, both constructive and deconstructive. Of the two major goals of this program, teaching self-awareness and teaching cognitive skills, by far the more difficult task is to teach self-awareness, and it requires feedback from as many sources as possible to achieve a broader effect.

In this chapter, I describe the methods that both parents and teachers can use to perform a "social autopsy" (Lavoie, 1994). There are two necessary aspects to evaluating an action. The child or adult needs to know how to perform a skill using all the steps that it entails (which I cover in Part Two, breaking the skills down into their basic components). But the more difficult aspect is to deconstruct the parts of the interaction with the child; you need to describe how you saw him performing the skill and to compare and contrast your perception with his own view of what occurred. Although it is easy to give positive feedback, giving constructive negative feedback as part of this deconstructive process is much more difficult. To give negative feedback in a positive way requires that you pay attention to the context (who else should hear the feedback, if anyone) and the quality of the relationship you have with the child who is receiving the feedback.

Who can hear the feedback on how the child with SN performed a new skill? If it is positive feedback, anyone can hear it. However, if the feedback is negative, I advise you to give it one-on-one. None of these children need to be embarrassed in front of their peers. The Hippocratic Oath is relevant here: "First, do no harm." Although teachers may wish to allow their SN students to role-play their newly acquired skills, teachers must remember that many of these children learn slowly, need lots of repetition, and have difficulty imagining and enacting how they would perform a new skill. In other words, they may not perform the skill well, which might embarrass them. The possible negative impact on their self-esteem are not worth the potential rewards, so **do not let children with SN participate in the role-playing exercises in front of their classmates, particularly for the more complicated exercises of joining a group or learning to handle teasing.** Let parents or a group leader (if they are in a social skills group) do these role-playing enactments with their children, either at home or in a small therapeutic group setting.

Parents and teachers can think of themselves as the football coach who jumps in to remind the children of a missed opportunity or to call attention to a positive play that an individual made. A coach often will let a player know how his move or play affected the whole team. Teachers have many opportunities to observe children and to provide this type of feedback. Again, the right time to give positive feedback is any time you see any child engaged in a positive interaction, whether it is in class, on the playground, on a field trip, or during an after-school activity. Whereas such praise as giving high-fives and saying "Great job" can be given in front of others, negative feedback should always be given privately.

The other way that parents and teachers coach children is by giving corrective feedback or helping them think of alternative behaviors. Who should give this type of negative feedback is determined by the relationship that exists with these children. Do they know and trust you and think that you are on their side? If they don't feel safe, negative feedback will be destructive. The goal of the teacher or parent is to always remind children of their positive qualities while giving negative feedback. I like to think of the parents and the teachers as the coach who has chosen these children because of their abilities and is just trying to help make them better at using specific skills. This is the meta-message that one needs to convey to these children when giving negative feedback.

Probing Steps to Deconstruct the Interaction

- Ask the child, "What caused the problem?"
- Check to make sure that you understand the answer.
- Role-play what you observed.
- Ask how it feels: Would the child like it if someone behaved this way toward him or her?
- Discuss alternative ways to handle the problem.

The goal of the deconstruction is for the parent or teacher to take the child aside and ask him how he saw his interaction with the other child. Does he know what he did? Does he see how it affected the other child? The adult asks him, "Do you know what you did? Can you think of another way you could have handled this?" Because many children with SN have perceptual problems, the adult may have to describe in detail what she observed.

There are many communication techniques that adults can use to help children increase their awareness of problematic interactions and come up with other possible ways they could have handled a difficult situation. Adults can:

- Coach children on alternatives by suggesting other desirable behaviors
- Probe to see how children describe the interaction from their perspective
- Restate or identify the behaviors that they observed
- Probe to see if children can identify alternative behaviors
- Ask questions that clarify or suggest alternative methods—for example, "What do you think would have happened if you had done ...?"
- Ask children to evaluate their alternatives by asking, "What do you think would have been the right way to handle this situation?"

Other good communication methods that fit into a coaching model address giving positive feedback and when necessary, minimizing mistakes. A good coach:

- Rewards positive change by praising children
- Draws attention to new, positive behaviors
- Ignores minor mistakes while focusing on positive behaviors
- Uses self-disclosure to minimize mistakes
- Uses humor privately (does not make fun of children in front of their peers)
- Reminds children that all skills get better with practice

Coaching Children on Desirable Behaviors

Perhaps the most effective way of coaching children in a new skill is to ask them what they already know about the skill. As the coach, you ask them to come up with alternative behaviors or to tell you what they could have done differently. Many of these children will not know what they did to create a problem. They may not see that they initiated an aggressive interchange or mistook a joke as a criticism. As the coach, you need to suggest alternative behaviors. In many instances, this requires that you also restate or identify all the behaviors that you have observed.

Strategies to Use to Encourage New Behaviors

- Use humor.
- Use self-disclosure.
- Model making mistakes.
- Reframe the problem.
- Coach the children on desirable behaviors.
- Ignore mistakes.
- Restate or identify behaviors observed.
- Ask clarifying questions.
- Draw attention to new, positive behaviors.
- Use praise.

Role Playing the Right Way Versus the Wrong Way

When children are stuck, one way to show them alternatives is to role-play the situation or problem. If a child is unaware of his negative behavior—for example, interrupting—I will often ask this child to demonstrate listening the "wrong way." The child who constantly interrupts will usually do an excellent job of demonstrating interrupting. This allows you to praise the child for doing the behavior that you want him to change. (This is called a "paradoxical intervention" in strategic family therapy.) Children love exaggerating and acting out the "wrong way," and it of course provides a great contrast to doing it the "right way."

Empathy: Being in the Other Person's Shoes

Many children with SN are unaware when they hurt someone else's feelings. To make and keep friends, they need first to be able to identify their own feelings and then recognize how the other person may feel. This edition of *Socially ADDept* includes a new lesson to help children increase their awareness and be more able to identify how people communicate their feelings through body language and tone (see Lesson Five).

Children benefit by role playing what it might look like to be in another person's shoes. Instead of being the one who said something mean, they pretend to be the recipient. The question is, "How did that feel?" For children with limited feeling language, give them four choices: "Did you feel sad, angry, annoyed, or hurt?" When children can identify how it felt, then the next step is for them to imagine how the other child might feel. As an example, "How does it feel when another child says something mean to you? Do you think that the other child might also feel sad, angry, annoyed, or hurt?" Because many of these children have not been able to focus on how other children feel, role playing being on the receiving end of negative comments is an invaluable teaching tool.

Empathy Checklist

- How does it feel to be on the receiving end of put-down teasing, aggression, or mean remarks?
- How do you think the other child feels?
- What could you do differently?

Using Humor

Because many children with SN misperceive humor and friendly teasing, it is important that adults be careful when using humor to correct any behavior. Children have to feel supported when they are corrected or reprimanded, so unless you have a very close relationship with a particular child, it is best to avoid using humor. Remember, many children with SN are very literal; they miss jokes and mistake friendly teasing as put-down humor and can be easily hurt by it. Instead of perceiving that you like them and are joking, they may feel you are making fun of them or rejecting them.

When alone with the child, a therapist or a parent might be able to exaggerate a child's mistakes (as in friendly teasing). It is important that this not be done in a classroom setting. Although the use of exaggeration is a form of friendly teasing, it should not be done by a classroom teacher because the child may misperceive it, or it may cause embarrassment. **It is only an effective strategy for parents, therapists, family friends, or those whom the child trusts** (and this method should not be used with children who cannot laugh at their mistakes).

Observing and Dealing with Perseveration

When children talk at great length (from two to ten minutes) on a subject or a topic of great personal interest to them, without any concern as to the reactions of the listener, the behavior is called *perseveration*. This kind of talking resembles a monologue or lecture and certainly is one-sided, because these children do not give the listener a chance to talk, comment, or change the topic (nor do these children pay attention to the listener's interest or lack thereof). Because most people expect to share a conversation, they want to avoid children (and adults) who perseverate.

Although you may not want to interrupt a child who is perseverating, pretending to listen when you are not doesn't teach the child to pay attention to the reactions of others. It is more valuable to say, "Sorry, I spaced out" or "I need some quiet time" or just "I'd rather talk about something else." Instead of being embarrassed that you are not following the "monologue" or are not interested, let the child know it is time to stop. Children need to learn how to judge the interest of their audience, and they need to learn that talking and listening are shared activities. When the other child is bored or not interested, children need to learn that they have to change the subject, listen, or stop talking and be quiet.

Make a contract with these children that if they are talking for more than forty-five seconds (without giving anyone else a chance to respond), you will give them a prearranged signal such as a time-out "T." Reward or praise them for stopping and letting another child talk or share her comments or ideas. If you are using a point system, these children should earn extra points for stopping when asked to do so.

Recess

Recess is a difficult time for many children with SN. During unstructured time, their lack of social skills is more apparent. They may not know how to join an ongoing group or game, or they may not know how to join a conversation without changing the subject or dominating. Their lack of coordination may make other children not want them as partners or to have them join their team. Often, children with SN find themselves alone during recess.

Some schools have adopted Circle of Friends, a program in which a child or a small group of children is recruited by the teacher or counselor to play with a less popular child for a specific period, such as lunchtime or recess. Although this type of program can serve as an introduction to a new group of children, if the child with SN does not know how to turn acquaintances into friends, the effect of Circle of Friends may not be lasting, as the child may still not know how to join a group or may think children who were recruited are really genuine friends (when they may not be).

Some schools have quiet places such as the library or computer room that are available during recess or lunch. Some children have a special relationship with a teacher and benefit from having specific chores to do. Giving these children an activity during recess can greatly reduce their anxiety, because free time is not perceived as "safe."

Cell phone or iPod use maybe be prohibited in classrooms or on the school grounds. However, for many children with SN, being able to connect with a friend outside of school is reassuring. Because texting a message on your cell phone does not rely on body language or tone, many children with SN use texting as a way to keep in touch with friends or acquaintances.

Monitoring Play

Teaching moments can happen any time an adult (parent, teacher, or professional) observes the identified child playing with others. Even when the children seem to be getting along, adults may need to intervene, particularly when the child says something hurtful, grabs a toy, or is physically aggressive. Because children are often unaware of how their behavior affects others, if you observe negative behavior, try to take the child aside and explain to her what you saw or heard—for example, that her tone was mean, that she grabbed the ball away, or that her remarks were hurtful. If you can catch the child "in action," she can frequently substitute an alternative behavior.

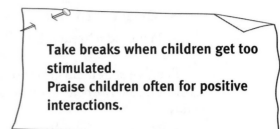

Take breaks when children get too stimulated.
Praise children often for positive interactions.

The play period is a great time to give positive praise. Praise children when you notice

- Sharing
- Friendly play
- Kind remarks
- Stopping when asked to do so by another

It is also appropriate to use time-out or ask them to take a break if they cannot control themselves or did not stop when asked.

Using Opportunistic Reinforcement

The best way to reinforce a new skill is to catch children while they are using the skill, which I call "catching them in action" (Giler, 1998a). It is the backbone of opportunistic reinforcement. Whenever you observe children using any of these new behaviors, *praise* them. If you see children sharing, listening, taking turns, and stopping when asked to do so during any free time (recess, lunchtime, free class time, or after-school activities), it is important to call attention to this desirable behavior. Although some programs emphasize charting these positive behaviors, it is just as effective to praise randomly or call attention to use of new behaviors or skills. Unlike friendly teasing, praising a child in front of other children highlights that the child has changed (De Shazer, 1991). This technique, called "news of difference," helps others see that the child has changed. Make a point of praising all new positive behaviors when they are observed. "Praise Early, Praise Often!"

Positive Behaviors to Reward

- Waiting
- Taking turns
- Listening without interrupting
- Making good eye contact
- Stopping when asked

Some Compliments to Use

- "Great listening."
- "Great eye contact."
- "You did a great job waiting and taking turns."

Positive statements that compliment children on their efforts are invaluable. Children love to hear such compliments as "You were really great at waiting today."

I cannot overstate that negative feedback should be given privately. Make sure that you do not correct children with SN in front of their classmates; they are likely to have low self-esteem, and it would be embarrassing to call attention to their flaws in front of others. You will forget the reprimand, but they may ruminate on it all day.

Chapter 3

Setting Individual Goals and Giving Structured Feedback

In this chapter, I discuss how to use structured feedback to help increase children's awareness of their behavior. The children define skills that they wish to acquire and then use the self-evaluation forms to evaluate their use of the skill(s). Children are prompted to fill out these forms by teachers or parents when they observe children using a new skill. The last step is for children to confer with an outside observer (parent or teacher) to confirm that their perception of their performance was accurate. This additional process requires children to figuratively step outside of their own frames of reference and begin to share a joint perception with the observer. The verification of joint perception helps children to see their behavior from someone else's point of view, one of the essential elements of being able to mind-read. Last, we look at other ways to monitor behaviors that are being charted.

Building Skills Teaches Resiliency

When children fail to make friends, it can affect both their attitudes and their self-concepts. Some children adopt negative attitudes. Some children stop trying altogether. They may say to themselves, "Why bother?" Children who give up may be unconsciously trying to protect themselves from failing and the injury to their self-esteem that failing would cause. (In "not trying," they can continue to hold the belief that if they had really tried, they could have succeeded; this belief, though perhaps untrue, protects their self-esteem. It has been called "positive illusory bias" and is defined as a defense mechanism that protects children from feelings of inadequacy.[1])

When the parent or teacher asks children with SN, "Why do you think it is hard to make friends?" they may reply with their belief that "there is something wrong with me." Their belief may be that they possess some character flaw that is the root cause of their problems. One of the cornerstones of the ADDept approach is to reframe the cause of their problems into something that they can control: it isn't their innate nature that is the problem; it is their lack of social skills, which they can acquire and which will enable them to able to interact in more socially acceptable ways.

Parents and teachers need to help children define the skills that they will need to succeed socially. As children begin this process of learning new skills, they often feel less overwhelmed because they see that making friends is a skill that they can acquire and that they will get better at with practice. Although this is true for most children, there are some children with SN who cannot shake their feelings of helplessness or hopelessness. Parents and teachers should refer children who appear depressed or who have excessive feelings of helplessness or hopelessness to mental health professionals for evaluation and treatment.

As children experience success making friends, they start to feel better about themselves. As mentioned in Chapter One, Erikson (1968) defined the developmental task of preadolescent children as *industry (competency) versus inferiority*. When children fail to master skills that their peers can do, they often feel self-doubt or have feelings of inferiority. When they begin to master social skills, they not only acquire friends but also increase their sense of self-worth.

Helping Children Set Their Goals

The first task is to define the social issue that is of greatest concern to each child. Although children may be struggling with being left out of a group at school, they may be more focused on the teasing they receive than on being left out of the group. When I have asked children, "Do you want to make more friends?" many, will say, "I have friends." A child will often deny that making friends is a problem, while his parent, who is sitting next to him, may catch my eye and shake her head in disagreement. I do not challenge the child's perception but rather shift the conversation by asking the child, "What would you like to see changed?" Most often, the child will want to stop the teasing. Whatever the child identifies as his major problem becomes our behavioral goal. I have often started therapy with a simple agreement to the question, "Would you want me to help you work on this so it doesn't happen anymore?"

Parents and teachers should ask the same question: "What do you want to see changed?" What children want to see changed becomes their therapeutic goal. The next task is to help children figure out what skills they need to learn to achieve their goal. Parents and adults need to help children review the different skills to define which skills are appropriate for each individual program.

It is important to remember that not all children will need all the lessons. Some children may not want nor need lots of friends. As introverts, they may be happier to deal with one child at a time and may only want one or two friends. They may not really want to be in large groups, so the lesson on how to join a group doesn't suit them and should be omitted. Another example is, a child who is already empathetic and reads body language and tone well doesn't need lessons that focus on these skills, so you might be able to skip Lesson Three or Lesson Five. The child's program should be individualized to incorporate the goals and skill level of each individual child.

Not everyone will use this book the same way. Each lesson has suggested discussions and activities that enable you to probe, teach, discuss, role-play, and reinforce new skills and behaviors. However, it can also be used as a reference book to gather information on a particular subject, such as how to deal with teasing or how to choose what the right response should be. It can also be used to look up specific issues, such as to whom to tell jokes and how children can use the rule of equals to judge if their audience is appropriate for a given joke. All the topics covered in the book are listed in the Index as well as in the Table of Contents.

Creating an Individual Program for Each Child

Adults need to familiarize themselves with the contents of this book to see how the lessons are laid out, referring to Figure 3.1, the Pyramid of Social Skills, and the ten lessons to help define which skills each child might need to acquire (see Chapter One). Although the book is laid out in a sequence, you should skip lessons that are not relevant for a particular child.

Figure 3.1 describes how these social skills are laid out in the lessons as building blocks or clusters of skills. At the base of the pyramid are the foundational skills of listening and responding and the other skills we use to engage in verbal conversations. The second tier introduces a cluster of nonverbal skills, such as how to read body language through facial expressions, gestures, and use of personal space. The third tier adds how tone modifies the words, introducing feelings and how they are expressed in tone, volume, speed, pitch, and so on. The fourth tier helps children recognize friendly body language and how to use this knowledge to know when to approach individuals or groups. The fifth tier introduces how to interpret discrepancies between the verbal and the nonverbal messages, and to understand which message takes priority. The sixth tier defines different forms of joking and teasing and suggests strategies that can be used to handle each form of teasing. Last, the seventh tier discusses anger management strategies, including dealing with meltdowns.

Figure 3.1 The Pyramid of Social Skills

Strategies to managing anger (and apologizing)

Strategies to handling teasing

Understanding humor (when the words and body language don't agree)

Reading friendly body language and using it to join a group

Tuning into feelings (tone, volume, speed, pitch)

Reading and using nonverbal body language (facial expressions, gestures and use of personal space)

The conversational skills: listening, greeting others, asking questions, giving compliments

Using the Self-Evaluation Forms

For every skill, you need to define four target behaviors that will be used to monitor the child's progress. These mini-goals, the target behaviors, are different for each skill. For example, if listening better is the child's first goal, you would monitor the four behaviors that are observable in people when they listen well (see Self-Evaluation Form: Listening on p. 41).

For the example of listening better, when you observe the child with SN listening to another boy or girl, you would ask her to fill out Self-Evaluation Form: Listening to reflect on and evaluate how well she performed the behaviors associated with good listening. The child rates herself on "How well did I listen?" using four characteristics. She gets one point for each of these behaviors that she used. The following are the four target behaviors related to listening; the child evaluates her listening by asking, Did I...

- Make good eye contact?
- Use interested body language?

- Refrain from interrupting or changing the subject?
- Ask questions, give compliments, or make comments?

The child gives herself a point for each behavior she thinks she did or consciously refrained from doing. The highest score she can get is a 4.

There are five self-evaluation forms included in this chapter. The forms evaluate different sets of skills: listening, showing interest, stopping when asked, controlling talking too much, and evaluating hosting behavior (see pp. 41–45). Each skill set has four behaviors that are used to evaluate the child's performance. Children rate themselves on how well they performed each set of skills, giving themselves a point for each positive behavior they did or negative behavior they did not do.

The parent's or teacher's job is likewise to rate the child on the behaviors that you may have observed. Children often think they did a great job and give themselves the maximum score of 4 points. You need to be ready to give corrective feedback, such as "You did a great job; however, do you remember that you interrupted Johnny? Because you interrupted, I would give you three points."

Although the self-evaluation forms are fairly simple, I have been surprised at how effective they appear to be. While leading ADDept groups, I often saw a surprising increase in the children's ability to accurately perceive their own behavior, often within the first five weeks of the ten-week program. I have postulated that this ability appears to lead to greater generalization of the learned social skills (Giler, 1998).

Using the Self-Evaluation Form to Confirm Joint Perception

While the child is filling out the self-evaluation form, the parent or teacher is also mentally reviewing the child's interaction to come up with her own rating of how well she thinks the child performed the skill (using the same four-point system). The last step measures the congruence between the child's perception and the external rating of the teacher or parent. If the adult and child both give the same score, it means that they both shared the same perception of the child's behavior. The child is rewarded by earning an additional point.

If the adult's assessment differs from the child's rating, the adult needs to specify why he disagreed with the child's assessment by recalling specific behaviors that he observed or naming behaviors that he thought were omitted. For example, the teacher could say, "You did a great job listening, except when you interrupted Mary while she was talking. Therefore, I'd give you three points instead of four." After a play date at home, the parent does the same process. When the child finishes evaluating his hosting skills (using Self-Evaluation Form: Being a Good Host on p. 45), the parent corrects his score by saying, "You did a great job hosting except when Mike wanted to stop playing and you kept playing until I came in and asked you to stop. Therefore I would give you three points instead of four."

The goal of comparing the two points of view is to teach children to accurately know which behaviors they did or did not do. Because many children were previously unaware of how they behaved, this process increases their abilities to self-assess and self-monitor. They also start to see interactions from someone else's point of view. Being able to compare their perceptions of their behavior with how someone else sees it helps them understand that other people see things differently than they do. Realizing that other people see, feel, think, and react differently than they do is a huge developmental step toward better perception of themselves and of others.

How the Self-Evaluation Forms Can Be Used to Create a Shared Perception (Joint Perception)

To acquire better joint perception, the child needs to

1. Perform the new skill (both the verbal and nonverbal aspects)
2. Accurately assess how well he performed the skill
3. Check with a neutral adult to see if the adult agrees with his assessment of how well he did it (sharing joint perception)

The objective of comparing the teacher's or parent's observation and rating with the child's perception and rating of her behavior is to enhance shared perception (joint perception; see Figure 1.2). This agreement matters more than the actual score (whether it is 4 points or 2) because the purpose of the comparison is to help the child see her behavior from another person's point of view. If the scores agree, the child is rewarded by earning an extra point. If the scores disagree, the adult perception is viewed as the more accurate, but the adult needs to supply information as to what he observed.

The Parent's Role as Facilitator

Parents need to monitor their children's progress and to coach and reinforce these new behaviors. The parent can give feedback in both structured and unstructured ways; both methods are valid. The parent can use a behavioral point system and can concurrently use opportunistic reinforcement (giving verbal praise with the intention of catching the child in action).

Likewise, it is important to reinforce any increase in self-perception, such as when children notice that they have interrupted, even if they were not able to stop themselves. It is also important to reinforce any new behavior, such as initiating a conversation with a new friend on the telephone or on the Internet or inviting another child over to play.

The parent's job is to

- Identify behaviors that will be needed for different tasks
- Discuss how to use the skills
- Mediate conflicts between children
- Identify what his or her child might be feeling
- Identify how the other child might feel
- Identify by hypothesizing what the intentions of the other child might be
- Identify alternative ways to handle the problem
- Help the child recover from refusals or disappointments
- Help the child find satisfying activities
- Help the child find supportive people

The Teacher's Role as Facilitator

The teacher's role is very similar to the parent's role, except that the teacher will have many more opportunities to see the child interact with others. Therefore, there will be more opportunities to stop negative interactions and to reward positive interactions. Many teachers are already charting behavioral goals, and if so, they can add more target behaviors to those that they are already charting. This chapter includes the self-evaluation forms already mentioned, a chart for negative behaviors, and a chart for positive behaviors.

Parents and Teachers Working Together

Although parents spend lots of time with their children, they do not see some of the problems that teachers see. It will help children if the parents and teachers meet so that they can both be working on the same goals and using similar strategies. It is important for both teachers and parents to realize that most parents are unprepared to teach social skills. Most parents have taught their children through modeling the appropriate behavior, a method that may not work well with children with SN. Parents and teachers need a framework to help them structure how they will impart social skills to children through setting goals and completing individual lessons and tasks.

Rewarding Progress

There are two basic methods for rewarding positive behaviors: opportunistic reinforcement, which we've already discussed, and behavioral charting.

Behavioral charting is an excellent way to reward changes. It requires that you give stars or points when you observe positive behaviors; you also need to have a reward system in place for redeeming the points. Please see the box "Behavioral Charting" at the end of the chapter for some ideas.

Another effective method is to use verbal comments and praise to reinforce the new behaviors. However, do not skip using the self-evaluation forms, as they are important aids to help children increase their ability to evaluate themselves. Further, when children make any progress toward understanding the feelings of others, or if they accurately take another person's perspective, it is important to notice and praise all attempts toward the desired behaviors, regardless of your method.

Correcting Omissions or Inappropriate Behaviors

The adult's role is to correct inappropriate behavior, particularly if a child is harming or hurting anyone else or displaying odd mannerisms, interrupting, being silly, or ignoring others when asked to stop. If a child is hurting someone else, you need to separate the children and give the offending child time-out. After the time-out is over, it is appropriate to ask the child why he hurt the other child and to see if he can think of ways he could have handled the situation differently.

If a child is doing an annoying behavior, use a nonverbal cue first to ask him to stop. If the child does not stop, use time-out. If you find after a week or two that a child persists in not stopping when asked to do so, the child might have an impulse problem that needs to be assessed by a professional.

Parents and teachers need to have some form of consistent behavioral management program in place to both reward positive behavior and to decrease negative behaviors. I often refer parents to *1,2,3, Magic* (Phelan, 2003) if they need help instituting a behavioral management program to change negative behaviors.[2] Adults need to use short and simple responses to negative behaviors and not engage in long discussions about omitted behaviors. The teaching moments for omitted skills should occur when children bring up problems or concerns, such as being teased at school or not being invited to a party.

NAME _____

Self-Evaluation Form: Listening

Child's Assessment

1. How well did I listen? Did I ...
   - Make good eye contact?
   - Use interested body language?
   - Refrain from interrupting?
   - Ask questions or make comments?

2. How well did I accomplish my goal(s)? How many behaviors did I do?

0	1	2	3	4
None	One	OK	Pretty well	Very well

Adult's Assessment

How well did the child accomplish his or her goal(s)? How many behaviors did I observe the child doing?

0	1	2	3	4
None	One	OK	Pretty well	Very well

The child gets an extra point if the child and the adult agree on how they rated the child's behavior.

NAME _____

Self-Evaluation Form: Showing Interest

Child's Assessment

1. How well did I show interest? Did I ...
   - Make good eye contact?
   - Lean forward?
   - Nod?
   - Ask questions or make comments?

2. How well did I accomplish my goal(s)? How many behaviors did I do?

0	1	2	3	4
None	One	OK	Pretty well	Very well

Adult's Assessment

How well did the child accomplish his or her goal(s)? How many behaviors did I observe the child doing?

0	1	2	3	4
None	One	OK	Pretty well	Very well

The child gets an extra point if both the child and the adult agree on the how they rated the child's behavior.

Self-Evaluation Form: Paying Attention to Stop Signs

Child's Assessment

1. How well did I pay attention to Stop signs? What did I do when the other person . . .
   - Used closed body language. Did I stop?
   - Rolled his or her eyes. Did I stop?
   - Used his or her hands to say "Stop." Did I stop?
   - Looked away repeatedly. Did I stop?
   - Looked annoyed. Did I stop?

2. How well did I accomplish my goal(s)? How many Stop signs did I see?

   0   1   2   3   4   5

   Did I stop?

   Not at all   Some   Totally stopped

Adult's Assessment

1. How many Stop signs did I observe?

   0   1   2   3   4   5

2. Did the child stop?

   Not at all   Some   Totally stopped

> The child can get two extra points in this exercise: one if both the child and the adult agree on how many Stop signs were observed, and one if both the child and the adult agree on whether or not the child stopped.

NAME _____

Self-Evaluation Form: Controlling Talking Too Much

Child's Assessment

This exercise is aimed at controlling talking too much and paying attention to how others tell you to stop.

1. Did I stop when I got the following Stop signals? What behaviors did I notice that told me to stop?
   - I noticed the child rolling his or her eyes.
   - I noticed that the child looked away repeatedly.
   - I noticed an annoyed look.
   - I noticed the child backing away.

2. How many Stop signs did I see?

        0   1   2   3   4

3. What did I do to stop?

     Stopped talking   Asked a question   Listened

Adult's Assessment

1. How many Stop signs did I observe?

        0   1   2   3   4

2. What did the child do to stop?

     Stopped talking   Asked a question   Listened

The child can get two extra points in this exercise: one if both the child and the adult agree on how many Stop signs were observed, and one if both the child and the adult agree as to how the child stopped.

NAME _____

Self-Evaluation Form: Being a Good Host

1. I was a good host. I did the following things:
   - ☐ I shared my toys.
   - ☐ I asked the other child what he or she wanted to do.
   - ☐ When the other child got bored, I stopped playing the game and asked the child what else he or she would like to do.
   - ☐ I put away toys I didn't want to share.

2. How many things did I do?

   0   1   2   3   4

Adult Assessment

How many behaviors did I observe?

0   1   2   3   4

> The child gets an extra point if both the child and the adult agree on how they rated the child's behavior.

Charting Negative Behavior

Charting is an effective method for helping children gain control over negative behaviors. It can help impulsive children who are unaware that they are annoying others. Annoying behaviors that can be included are interrupting, making noise, failing to respect someone's space, rocking, making funny gestures, name-calling, or not stopping when asked. Although positive behavioral reinforcement is generally preferable, sometimes children need to increase their awareness of their negative behaviors. I do not recommend using this method for more than three weeks, because it's more desirable to measure the absence of negative behaviors than their presence. As mentioned previously, if the child cannot control negative behaviors (meaning you see no decline in negative events while charting), it is possible that the problem is one of impulsiveness.

Behavior	Mon	Tues	Wed	Thurs	Fri	Sat	Sun
Interrupting							
Making noise							
Violating space							
Name-calling							
Using odd gestures							

Charting Positive Behavior

After the third week of charting negative behavior, switch to noting both positive behaviors as well as the absence of negative behaviors. It is of course harder to notice the absence of annoying behaviors, but because you already charted them, you will have a good idea of how many incidents occur within a week.

For example, suppose that the child was interrupting or making noise an average of three to five times a day during the previous three weeks. Now, you notice that the number has dropped to two times a day. Give the child points for controlling being annoying. Give the child points for being good.

Behavior (+)	Mon	Tues	Wed	Thurs	Fri	Sat	Sun
Listening							
Making eye contact							
Smiling							
Using friendly body language							
Asking questions							

Giving compliments
Stopping when asked
Offering to help
Controlling anger outbursts
Behavior (−)
Not interrupting
Not making noise
Not violating space
Not name-calling
Not using odd gestures

The child gets one point for each time he or she performs a positive behavior or refrains from exhibiting a negative behavior. Try to catch the child being good by noting the absence of negative behaviors.

For ideas about redeeming points, see the box "Behavioral Charting."

Behavioral Charting

Behavioral charting is an excellent method that many parents and teachers like to use. It depends on consistency, and some find that it is difficult to keep going to the chart to record points. Another method is to carry around pennies or chips and give the child a basket or jar to put them in. The child can count the points up at the end of the day or week. Adults need to make clear to the child how he or she can redeem the points for rewards. Possible rewards you might offer are listed here.

If the child can earn 25 to 50 points in a week, rewards could be

- Money, allowance
- Free-time activities (computer or Internet time, cell phone time)
- Renting a computer game
- Having a friend over
- Going out for dinner or snacks
- Getting to play Nintendo or a Wii game

The child might aim to earn 100 to 200 points over a longer period (one to two weeks). Possible incentives could be

- Going to a special place (bowling alley, ice skating, skateboard park)
- Seeing a movie
- Playing miniature golf

(continued)

(continued)

If your child aims for a high number of points (300 to 500), special treats could include

- Taking a fishing trip, camping, or going on an outing with a friend
- Going to an amusement park or getting a ticket to watch a favorite team play
- Attending a concert

For more information on behavioral reward systems, see Parker (1996).

Notes

1. Several studies have consistently found that children with ADHD demonstrate a "positive illusory bias" (PIB), defined as a disparity between self-report of competence and actual competence, such that self-reported competence is significantly higher than actual competence (Hoza, Pelham, Dobbs, Owens, & Pillow, 2002). This bias is assumed to be self-protective, as the child hides his social incompetencies to protect himself from feelings of failure or inadequacy. This inflating of his perception of his competence functions as a self-protective defense mechanism (Ohan & Johnston, 2002; Hoza et al., 2002; Owens, Goldfine, Evangelista, Hoza, & Kaiser, 2007). The authors think that children with other disabilities, such as learning disabilities, Nonverbal Learning Disability, and Asperger's Syndrome, may also exhibit PIB (or the converse, deflated illusory biased self-perception). In laymen's terms, this means that children perceive themselves as having more skills than they actually do (or conversely, fewer skills). In either situation, the child's self-perception is skewed. Accurate self-perception is the foundational skill that children need to acquire so that they can use the more interactive skills of joint perception and mind reading.

2. Dr. Phelan's DVD is available in English and Spanish. His method relies on outlining clear behavioral principles for changing behavior. He suggests that a core mistake is parents' belief that their children need to like the discipline that the parents use. Because of this belief, parents engage in too much talking, explaining, and negotiating.

Chapter 4

Ways Parents Can Help

One of the most important jobs parents have is to make sure their children have healthy self-esteem. Self-esteem is based on a child's recognition of her positive traits and on her acquisition and mastery of age-appropriate skills. As a parent, you can be a cheerleader, but it is also important for you to steer your child into activities in or out of school, whether the activity is a sport or sharing a specific skill such as music or art. Your child needs to be steered toward activities where he can begin to use his skills to make friends (see Lesson One, Exercise 8: Finding Neighborhood Activities: The Parent's Job).

Helping Your Child Find and Excel in an Activity

Because children's self-esteem relies on their ability to master a skill, it is important that parents find activities in which their children experience success. It doesn't matter whether the activity is in school or out, or whether the activity is exclusively with children their own age. What matters is that children socialize with others and that they start to feel competent.

You need to find an activity that suits both your child's interests and his ability. Some children will excel in music, art, or theater. Some children are naturally coordinated and excel in team sports, but if your child isn't well coordinated, he is better off in sports that don't require team participation, such as martial arts, gymnastics, dancing, hiking, biking, swimming, boating, fishing, horseback riding, surfing, diving, or golfing. Many of these activities can be shared with children and adults of all ages.

If your child is musical, learning to play an instrument can allow him to participate in an orchestra or band, which can enable him to be part of group where social skills are less significant. Likewise, if your child sings well, she can participate in a choir. Musical training can also help teach children how to fit in, take turns, listen to the others, and harmonize, because children have to follow the leader's tempo, pacing, volume, and intensity. Children need these skills to distinguish how they and others use tone. (See Lesson Five.)

Joining a theater production is another great way for the child to be part of a group. For some children, acting comes very easily. Acting can teach emotional expression, as facial expressions, tone, inflection, and body language are all exaggerated for the audience. Being in a play also involves waiting and taking turns. A wonderful theater project was the subject of the HBO film *Autism: The Musical.* The film tracked a small group of children throughout the year as they prepared to put on a play. The uplifting stories of the children and their social progress that resulted from their participation in the theater production were heartwarming. (This film is available through Netflix or at www .autismthemusical.com.)

Preparing for Social Situations

Your role is to plan and monitor social activities for the preschool and early elementary school–age child. To prepare your child for the get-together, he needs to know what "good hosting" behavior is. You also need to monitor the activities from a distance (such as in another room where you can overhear their play). When your child is in fourth or fifth grade, he will need help with planning and figuring out which child to invite over and what the activities will be. If your child does not have close friends by fourth grade, he should be in a social skills group.

Setting Up the Initial Social Contact

If your child is under eight or nine years of age, most of the arrangements for play dates, visits, or sleepovers are initiated or coordinated by you and the other child's parent(s). Before you invite a child over, make sure that your child is aware of what behaviors are expected of her and that you have discussed sharing toys; also be sure to have put away any toys that will not be shared. It is important to have structured activities available. The initial play date should be for about two hours. Make sure that you have clearly explained this to the other parent. You need to be available to monitor the children's activities from another room. The goal is to make sure the get-together goes well and that the visiting child will want to play with your child again.

A good strategy is to ask the parent if her child can bring over a favorite game or toy to share. If the children share an interest, such as collecting toy characters, it is a good idea to plan something that involves these characters.

Other possible first-time activities can be drawing; painting; playing with clay or play dough, board games, micro-machines, Legos™, or dolls; imaginary play with costumes or forts; or a sports game, such as basketball, table tennis, or air hockey.

Because entertaining often involves sharing food, it is important to have some favorite snacks available. You might want to ask the child's parent what the child's favorite foods are so that you can have some available. Or perhaps you can do a cooking activity, such as baking and decorating cookies. The important thing to convey to your child is that being a good host means playing what the other child wants to play and changing activities when the other child wants to change. Noninteractive toys, such as movies, DVD games, and computer games, are not good for encouraging interactions and should not be used during an initial play date. If movies, DVD games, and computer games are going to be off-limits, make sure to remind your child of this before the play date occurs.

Discussing the Rules for Being a Good Host

Well before the play date, be sure to explain to your child the rules for being a good host. Begin by saying, "Your job is make sure the other child has a good time and wants to come back over to play with you again."

Rules for Being a Good Host

- Always ask the other child what he or she would like to do, and try to do that activity or game.
- Always let the child play with your toys. (If something is off-limits, you put it away beforehand.)
- Always give your guest foods that he or she likes.
- Always stop playing a game when your guest wants to play something else.

Although these rules are simple and easy to follow, many parents don't think about them before the guest comes over. I remember my son going over to a friend's house where he was told not to touch any of the boy's toys. (Needless to say, my son didn't want to go over there to play again.) Fighting over a special toy can be avoided by just putting the toy away ahead of time.

Using Discipline During a Play Date

If you notice that your child is being mean or aggressive, it is appropriate to separate the children and give your child a time-out. Because resolving conflicts is not a skill many children with SN have, you should be available to help them work out any conflicts by reminding them to share, suggesting how they might compromise, or redirecting them to a different activity. Sometimes just taking breaks or doing something more physical will work out the problems. If it is obvious that the children are not getting along, you may want to let them watch TV or a DVD until the other parent comes to pick up his or her child.

Preparing Children for New Situations

Because most children with SN do not like change, any transition to a new situation can be difficult. They may see the new situation as scary, and they may have anxiety about what to expect. To help reduce anxiety, you need to arrange a visit to a new school or camp before it starts. (Many schools or camps have a visitors day for new children.) You can ask the teacher or camp director for names of other new children or to see if he or she can assist you in arranging a meeting between the new children. It is helpful to talk to the teacher, principal, or camp director and explain that your child may need a little extra assistance in making this transition. If a child is extremely anxious, cognitive-behavioral therapies (such as Eye Movement Reprocessing and Desensitization, or EMDR) can be useful to manage or reduce anxiety.

Teaching Manners

Teaching manners, or etiquette, the culturally agreed-on rules that make social interactions easier, seems to be less prevalent these days. More children are exposed to television ads and seem to copy the sexy teenager in the commercial who gobbles a hamburger while catsup drips down his face and shirt. Although Emily Post's version of etiquette may be a thing of the past, it is still true that popular children have good manners. They wait their turn, they invite others to join them in activities, they smile and greet others, they give compliments and thank people for assisting them, and they have a neat appearance (and usually don't talk with their mouths full of food unless they cover their mouths with their hands!).

Children with SN need to learn and practice good manners, as they are less likely to notice the gasp, groan, or disgusted look from anyone watching them do something unacceptable, and they are far less likely to correct their behavior on cue. Popular children can perceive when they have gone too far and can address their poor manners with humor or an apology, but children with SN often don't see that they are making someone else uncomfortable. Therefore it is easier to go back to Emily Post and teach them basic good manners. Even if some people have become more lax about such things as talking with their mouths full, others will find such behavior offensive (and children still need to know how to use knives and forks). Although this might not be an issue with their peers, it can be a problem for them when they are in more formal social situations, such as when they are eating in restaurants or attending formal receptions like a wedding.

If your child goes on automatic pilot when he eats, use a mirror so that he can see himself during the meal. Reward him for positive table manners, such as using utensils properly, not talking with his mouth full, and using simple phrases such as "Please" and "Thank you" (while making eye contact) when he asks for items to be passed to him.

Building Physical Coordination

Cratty (1996) has estimated that 30 to 50 percent of children with learning disabilities have coordination apraxia (meaning they have trouble coordinating their muscle movements). This can also be true for other children with SN. Their lack of coordination can make these children unpopular picks for team sports, so they need to have alternative activities. All activities that increase coordination but can be done at the child's pace, such as swimming, gymnastics, martial arts, golfing, or bike riding, are good choices.

Children with coordination problems can be helped by therapies and physical activities that focus on coordinating the sensory motor system. Ayers (1972) developed a system called sensory-motor integration for children who have coordination problems. Children who have severe coordination problems are often referred to occupational therapists for intensive therapy. Encourage your child to do these activities, even if he is clumsy and hates to do physical exercise. Your child's coordination will improve with effort. Lara (2009) has developed a funny DVD to teach children who have Asperger's Syndrome hip-hop dance. (In the DVD, she shows them how to use their robotic movements to their advantage.) All forms of dance, yoga, and gymnastics will improve coordination as well (Lande, 1999; Rosenholtz, 1993).

Most boys love computer games. They like being in control and being able to act out aggressions or fantasies of power. There are some benefits to computer games; they can improve eye-hand coordination, and the newest generation of games for the Nintendo Wii console (and PlayStation) actually require player(s) to coordinate their physical motions so that they can produce actions on the television or computer screen. Similarly, *Dance Dance Revolution* works by having the child stand on a sensor that picks up his footsteps while he attempts to duplicate the dance movements that are choreographed on the screen. In all these games, the feedback is immediate.

Even though these types of computer or DVD games may have a therapeutic effect, children are now playing these games on average in excess of fifteen hours a week. Video or computer gaming addiction is a new mental health diagnosis and can lead to increased violence or a distorted view of reality. Children's use of video games should not replace their interactions with others or their participation in sports, music, and the arts.

Helping Children Learn About Time

Although teaching about time is slightly outside the scope of learning social skills, it is nevertheless important because many children with ADHD do not have good internal clocks. They can easily lose thirty minutes (if not an hour).

"Spacing out" can make a short assignment very time consuming, or they may be late for school or an after-school group activity. (Many will be disorganized as well and will misplace their homework or knapsack. Make it a habit to have your child put his knapsack and homework by the door before he goes to bed. See Hallowell and Ratey, 1994, for more tips on organization and time management.)

Children (particularly those with ADHD) do best in highly structured environments that are consistent enough that the child can learn to predict what will happen next. Make a chart of the activities that your child needs to do in the morning, after school, and after dinner. (You can use pictures if that is more suitable for your child.) Activities or events that can occur at the same time each day include waking up, getting ready for school, coming home from school, attending scheduled after-school activities, play time, dinner time, homework time, free time after doing homework, and preparing for bed and bedtime. (Another tip for parents of children who take medication: wake your child up thirty minutes earlier to allow time for the medication to kick in before he has to start his morning rituals of getting ready for school.)

Many arguments can be avoided if you do not let your child play computer games or watch TV before school or before doing homework. Most children do not want to stop playing their computer games or watching television, as these are highly interesting and engrossing activities. Parents are encouraged to use computers time or television as rewards for completing homework.

Using Humor Appropriately

As we've discussed elsewhere, children with SN can make mistakes understanding humor, often overreacting to a friendly tease because they don't know how to distinguish it from put-down humor. They may also tell inappropriate jokes (about character flaws) or use bathroom humor that may offend their audience. This is an important subject to discuss with your child, who may not know the hidden rules of humor. Children are often teased for making inappropriate jokes, and if they don't stop, other children assume that they are "weird" or "odd" or just insensitive. In this edition, there are two new sections on humor in Lesson Eight: 8.9, When Jokes Aren't Funny; and 8.10, The Rule of Equals. These sections describe how to tell a joke and to whom to tell it.

Finding a Social Skills Group

Although you may feel your child's frustration and pain, you might not know what to do about it. Unlike her siblings, the child with SN may not learn by imitating or by copying her peers (including brothers and sisters). In other words, it isn't your fault for not modeling the appropriate skills; your child needs specific instruction and coaching.

If your child is over eight years old and is having trouble making a "best friend," or you notice that he is being excluded from class birthday parties, it is time to find a group. I believe children learn best by being in small, therapeutic groups of four to six children who are close in age and have similar issues

Many children with SN are covered under IDEA and the Americans with Disabilities Act, section 504. If your child is receiving services at a public school and has an IEP (Individualized Educational Program) or a 504 plan, you can request that she participate in a social skills group at her school. If you prefer to have your child participate in a group outside of school, check with your local support groups to see if there are any social skills groups available. Many parents have found that if they approach a local psychologist, marriage and family therapist, or social worker, this individual is often willing to start a social skills group (particularly if you supply the curriculum).

Most social skills groups use some version of structured learning (McGinnis, Goldstein, Sprafkin, & Gershaw, 1984). The groups need to (1) teach social rules and expectations and the steps necessary to execute the skill, (2) use modeling and rehearsal of alternative ways to manage social situations, (3) coach the children on their use of the new skills, and (4) have some means for children to evaluate their performance of the skills so as to enhance their self-perception (Giler, 1998a).

Meeting Other Parents

All parents can benefit from support, but the parents of children with SN can benefit from finding others who are struggling with similar parental issues. There are many support groups for each specific problem. These groups offer parents the opportunity to meet other parents, share solutions to common problems, and share resources, such as information about the best schools or doctors in your area. Most parents find that meeting other parents normalizes their experiences, makes their challenges easier, and often alleviates their feelings of isolation. Recommended support groups are listed in the Bibliography and Resources.

Getting Help for Yourself

Children with SN are challenging for most parents, and particularly for a parent who shares a similar disability. It is easier for the parent who doesn't have a similar problem to be calmer or more objective. Sometimes parents with similar problems find that they unconsciously resent the help or attention that their children are getting; they may also be more impatient without realizing it. Some parents learn of their own disability during their child's assessment process. For many parents, it can explain why their own life has been so difficult. Because many of these problems run in families, there is usually someone else in the family who has a similar problem.

One of the hardest things for parents to accept is that there is something wrong with their child. It is common to be very angry at the teacher or other school personnel when they tell you that your child needs to be assessed for a specific impairment. Most parents' first reaction is to deny there is a problem or to be angry at the messenger. If you (or your spouse) is having trouble accepting a diagnosis, you are encouraged to seek professional counseling. The principal or school psychologist may suggest a therapist or counselor, or you can search the Web for therapists or psychologists who work with families with specific disabilities.

Sometimes a child's parents do not equally accept that there is a problem; one may know that something is wrong, but the other may refuse to accept it or may suggest that the spouse is somehow to blame, often citing the spouse's overly indulgent method of child rearing or discipline. If you and your spouse do not agree and it is affecting your marriage, it is best to discuss your differences with a trained marital therapist, counselor, or psychologist.

Part II

The Socially ADDept Lessons

Friendship Skills and Setting Goals

Children don't usually think about what qualities make people friends. They only pay attention to the fact that they have friends or that they aren't friends with someone anymore. Frequently, they don't know why someone stopped being friends with them. In this lesson, you ask the child, "What are friends? What are the skills that people use to make and keep friends?" This lesson introduces the idea that making and keeping friends are skills that children can learn.

1.1   What Makes a Friend?

Ask:

What makes people friends?
What do you like about your friends?

Write down what the child says.
Then reiterate or add the following:

- We like children who show concern (caring).
- We like children who play with us.
- We like children who listen to us.
- We like children who share with us.
- We like children who laugh with us.
- We like children who have similar interests.

1.2 What Do Friendly People Do?

Initiate a conversation about what social behaviors popular or friendly children use.

Say:

> *Think about the popular children in your school class. Do you know what they do that makes people like them? It turns out that friendly people do some things in common. Can you guess what friendly people do?*
>
> *Do they greet you and smile?*
>
> *Do they ask you how your day is?*
>
> *Do they listen to you when you talk?*
>
> *Do they share their thoughts, feelings, or belongings with you?*

If appropriate, refer to "What Do Popular Children Do?"

What Do Popular Children Do?

- They may greet you by name and smile.
- They initiate conversations, ask questions, and show interest.
- They extend invitations.
- They give compliments.
- They share.
- Their appearance is good.
- They listen to you when you talk.
- They share their thoughts, feelings, or toys.

★ **Assign Exercise 1:** What Do Friendly People Do?

1.3 Ten Friendship Skills

Ask: *Do you know what skills friends use with each other?*
Answers might include the following:

They listen.

They smile and use friendly body language.

They show people they care about them.

They remember things that are important to their friends.

They invite people to events.

They share.

They solve problems.

They compromise.

Review the box "Ten Essential Friendship Skills" and add any skills missed to the list you started.

By introducing the concept that making friends is a skill, you begin the process of empowering the child. If making friends is a skill, then she can learn how if she practices.

Ten Essential Friendship Skills

1. Greet others (use their names, smile, make eye contact).
2. Listen and respond (share).
3. Show interest (ask questions, make comments).
4. Give compliments (extend invitations).
5. Understand and use appropriate body language and tone of voice.
6. Respect personal space and use appropriate touching.
7. Join ongoing activities with peers.
8. Solve problems and conflicts.
9. Handle teasing and friendly joking.
10. Manage anger and apologize when necessary.

1.4   Defining Personal Goals

Ask the child to construct personal goals using Exercise 2: Defining My Personal Goals.

Ask:

Do you want to learn any of these skills?

Which skills do you want to learn?

From this conversation, you can help the child clarify and construct what his or her goals are.

1.5   Defining Positive Qualities

Say:

We all have qualities that we like about ourselves. I want you make a list of the things you like about yourself. We'll call this list "Positive Self-Talk"—"positive," because it focuses on what you like about yourself, and "self-talk," because this is a private dialogue that you have with yourself. I want you to create a list of things that you like about yourself.

Sometimes people criticize themselves for what they didn't do well. This is called negative self-talk. Instead of focusing on your faults, it's time to start a new habit of daily reminding yourself of the things that you like about yourself. You will want to keep these thoughts to yourself because telling others what you like about yourself is considered to be bragging, which is not socially acceptable to others.

Make sure the child understands the difference between what he says or thinks to himself (whether it's positive "self-talk" or thinking something mean about another person) versus saying it out loud to someone else. Does the child understand the difference between his personal thoughts and what he shares with others (public statements)? It is important to stress this difference because what a person says and does creates consequences or reactions in others.

> **Keep positive self-talk to yourself — don't BRAG.**

Say:

> *Do you understand the difference between your personal thoughts and feelings and what you should share with others? A good example is that you can think someone is fat, but if you say to him, "Gee, you're fat," you will more than likely hurt his feelings; the person probably won't want to be your friend and may, in fact, want to turn people against you.*

Discuss this social rule: "You can think or feel anything, but what you say and do creates reactions in others."

★ **Have the child do Exercise 3:** Tooting Your Own Horn.

If the child needs some examples of positive qualities, refer to the box "Positive Self-Talk."

> **Social Rule: You can think or feel anything, but what you say and do creates reactions in others.**

There are two types of positive strokes children can give themselves: they can describe qualities that they possess or things that they do well. Both are important, so encourage the child to come up with examples of each. If the child needs help, you can give examples of what qualities, traits, or gifts you have noticed about her.

Say:

> *Everyone has ideas about herself that she keeps in her mind. Sometimes it is useful to write down these qualities and abilities so that when you are feeling bad about yourself, you can remember your positive qualities.*

Review "Positive Self-Talk" if you haven't already.

Positive Self-Talk

Qualities	Skills
I'm a good person.	I'm good at cooking.
I'm very smart.	I'm good at _____ sport.
I'm a good and loyal friend.	I'm a good writer.
I work very hard.	I'm a good actor.
I'm very honest.	I'm good with computers.
I'm very creative.	I'm handy at fixing things.
I'm funny.	I'm good at painting.
I'm helpful.	I'm good at singing.

Just in case the child is having a difficult time coming up with qualities that she likes about herself, you can refer to the box "Children with SN: A Different Kind of Mind," which lists some very special qualities that children with SN have. Be aware, however, that not all traits are equally present in all children with SN—for example, children with Asperger's Syndrome might have problems with empathy, whereas some children with learning disabilities are exceptionally empathetic.

Children with SN: A Different Kind of Mind

The following are positive qualities that children with SN may possess:

- Rapid grasp of concepts
- Awareness of patterns
- Energy
- Curiosity
- Incredible concentration when interested
- Exceptional memory for certain details
- Empathy (not a strength for all children with SN)
- Vulnerability and openness
- Heightened sensory perception
- Divergent thinking

1.6   Identifying Children's Special Interests

Because we frequently make and keep friends who share similar interests, it is also important to be able to identify what children like to do in their spare time. It is also useful for parents to figure out what their children do well. Ask:

What do you like to do in your spare time?
★ Homework for children:

- Ask the child to do Exercises 5 and 6.
- Parents and teachers need to work out a signal with the child that means STOP.
- Ask the child to think of new activities that he would like to try.

★ Homework for parents:

- Name three positive qualities that you like about your child.
- Name three things that you do well as a parent.
- Look for positive things to say to your child.
- Introduce the concept of how to be a good host and review the rules with your child (see Exercise 7).
- Start scouting out places in the community to find children who share similar interests with your child (see Exercise 8: Finding Neighborhood Activities).

Exercise 1: What Do Friendly People Do?

For each of the following situations, check the box that describes how the person is acting. Do you think it is friendly or unfriendly behavior? If you aren't sure, check "Not Sure."

A person passes you on the street, looks you in the eye, and smiles and nods.

    ☐ Friendly   ☐ Not Sure   ☐ Unfriendly

You see a kid you know, and he looks sad. You go over to talk to him.

    ☐ Friendly   ☐ Not Sure   ☐ Unfriendly

When you see someone you know, you say "Hi" quickly and look away.

    ☐ Friendly   ☐ Not Sure   ☐ Unfriendly

When a friend wants to tell you about a new game, you change the subject because you are jealous.

    ☐ Friendly   ☐ Not Sure   ☐ Unfriendly

A child in your class brings her dog to school. You go over and ask questions, such as "Can I pet him?"

    ☐ Friendly   ☐ Not Sure   ☐ Unfriendly

Exercise 2: Defining My Personal Goals

The purpose of this exercise is to help you think about what you would like to have be different in your life. Circle any of these statements if they reflect your own goals, or add your own:

- To make friends

- To listen better

- To keep friends

- To join ongoing activities

- To give compliments

- To share and play better

- To handle teasing

- To use friendly body language

- To invite children over

- To remember what is important to my friends

- To manage anger better

- To cooperate more

- To be more positive

- To _____
  _____

- To _____
  _____

- To _____
  _____

Exercise 3: Tooting Your Own Horn

Everyone has qualities that he likes about himself. These qualities are the basis of self-esteem. This exercise asks you to name your personal positive qualities and also add the things that you think you do well. Here are examples of positive qualities (called positive affirmations).

Circle the ones that fit you:

I'm good at _____ .

I'm a good person.

I'm very smart.

I'm a good and loyal friend.

I work very hard.

I'm very honest.

I'm very creative.

I'm funny.

I'm helpful.

Add things you like about your physical appearance:

I like my hair.

I like my nose.

Now make your own list:

I do _____ well.

I'm good at _____ .

_____

_____

_____

_____

_____

_____

_____

Exercise 4: Private or Public Talk?

Some of the things you think about or that happen in your life are private, and you should not share that information with other people.

In this exercise, for each situation, show whether it is something that you can share with others or that you should keep private.

Your family got a new 3D TV.	Keep Private	Share
Your dad lost his job.	Keep Private	Share
You know a secret about someone.	Keep Private	Share
You love your new haircut.	Keep Private	Share
You got a 100 on the test.	Keep Private	Share

Write down two things that you know about your family that you should keep private.

_____

_____

Exercise 5: Identify Your Interests

Fill in the blanks with activities you like to do.

What do you do after school? _____

What sports do you like to play? _____

What's your favorite computer game? _____

What kind of movies do you like? _____

What books do you like to read (magazines, comics, and so on)?

_____

_____

Name five activities that you like to do for fun:

_____

_____

_____

_____

_____

Name any school clubs or after-school organized activities that you do or would like to do—for example, team sports, individual sports, local theater, art class, cooking class, band, choir, orchestra, computer clubs:

_____

_____

_____

_____

_____

Exercise 6: Friendship Cards: Keep a Record of Facts About Your Friends

Sometimes we don't pay attention to things that are important to our friends—or we just forget. In this exercise, you will make up a separate card for each current or potential friend. You'll keep these cards and update them. They will help you keep track of things that are important to your friends. You can use blank index cards, or you can make a page for each friend in a journal. You want to write down everything you know about each person.

What does he or she do after school? _____

What sports does he or she like to play? _____

What kinds of music does he or she like? Who is his or her favorite singer or group? _____

What is his or her favorite TV show?

_____

What movies has he or she seen and mentioned liking (or hating)?

_____

What does he or she like to read (magazines, comics, and so on)?

_____

Name five activities that he or she does for fun:

_____

_____

Name any school clubs or after-school organized activities that he or she does—for example, team sports, individual sports, classes, local theater, religious school classes, band, choir, orchestra, computer clubs:

_____

_____

Names of his or her siblings or anyone else who lives with him or her (cousins, stepsiblings): _____

Name of his or her favorite pet: _____

Exercise 7: Good Host Rules

Note: This is a parent-child exercise.

This is the start of an ongoing discussion with your child. Introduce the topic and what the rules will be; go over these rules again before your child invites a child over and before the guest arrives. You may have to repeat them a number of times, as it often takes many repetitions to learn new behaviors.

Rules for Being a Good Host

- Always ask the other child what he or she would like to do and try to do that activity or game.

- Always let the child play with your toys (if something is off-limits, you can put it away beforehand).

- Always give your guest foods that he or she likes.

- Always stop playing a game when your guest wants to play something else.

Exercise 8: Finding Neighborhood Activities: The Parent's Job

Note: This exercise is for parents only.

- You need to search out activities in your neighborhood. Use the Internet or the local paper to find such activities (see list). Cities often have a Department of Parks and Recreation that runs recreational programs that might be interesting to your child.

- Make an agreement that your child will try out an activity at least two times. If she agrees to join the activity, she needs to make a commitment to stay with it for a year or a season.

- Make an agreement that your child will take the activity seriously and not goof off or be distracting.

- While your child is participating in the activity, you need to be there and unobtrusively observe if there are any children with whom your child seems to get along (or any parents who seem likeable or approachable).

- While your child is involved in the activity, you need to talk to the other parents who are there. Note parents who are new in town or who appear friendly.

- While observing your child in the activity, if you notice that he seems to like another child, ask him after the activity is over whether he would like to try to get together with this child. If the answer is yes, you need to talk to the other child's parent (or caregiver) and get their contact information.

- If your child is over eight or nine, ask her if she would like (1) to invite the child over, (2) to call the other child on the telephone and invite her over or (3) to invite the other child over at the end of the next scheduled meeting.

- If your child is under nine and uncomfortable asking another child over, your job is to ask the other parent if your children can get together. You arrange this on the telephone or after the next scheduled meeting.

- If your child is over eight and doesn't have good telephone skills, you need to rehearse how to use the phone. She needs to learn to (1) introduce herself and (2) make it clear to the other person why she is calling (for example, she needs homework information or wants to invite the child to some event). Have your child rehearse making a telephone call with you or have her practice by calling a family friend or relative. For more information on this topic, see *Good Friends Are Hard to Find* (Frankel, 1996), specifically the chapter titled "Using the Telephone to Make Closer Friends."

- Remember to discuss good hosting behavior before the other child comes over (see Exercise 7).

Search local newspapers and the Internet for other activity ideas.

Boy or Girl Scouts	Computer gaming clubs
Boating	Art classes
City sports teams	Comic collectors groups
Dance	Cooking classes
YMCA	Jewelry making
Gymnastics	Pottery classes
Martial arts classes	Other crafts
Yoga classes	Scuba diving
Theater productions	Fishing
Archery	Fencing
Horseback riding clubs	Kick boxing
Coin collectors	Hiking
Music groups	Mountain biking

Also consider volunteer activities: museum, hospitals, nursing homes, food banks, and shelters.

Being a Good Listener and Other Conversational Skills

When children get together, they spend time playing, and interspersed with their play, they talk, joke, and in general share what's on their minds. Many children think that talking is the most important part of the conversation, but it is the act of listening and responding that makes other children feel valued. Many children with SN fail to respond to what the other child says (through words or body language), which encourages the other child to seek out other friends who appear more interested or concerned. Learning how to respond to another person is the topic of this lesson.

2.1 Listening

When we meet someone new, we spend about 55 percent of our time listening. Through listening and asking questions, we learn what is important to the other person. Although many children with SN actually do listen to others, many of them fail to respond. Some of the mistakes that children with SN make include

- Failing to listen without interrupting
- Not acknowledging they have heard what the speaker said
- Responding by changing the topic of conversation
- Responding by talking about themselves

Because listening is such an important skill, make sure that you discuss both why listening is important and how to listen well. Many children with SN think listening is a passive activity, but children who are good at listening are very active. (They nod, make comments, ask questions, and so on.) Responding to others with words or gestures confirms that you

> Listening has two parts: You have to listen, and you have to respond with gestures or words or sounds like "Uh huh."

- Have heard him or her
- Are following what he or she is saying
- Are interested in what he or she is saying

Ask:

How do you show a person that you are listening?

Write down what the child says, and if you have her demonstrate how she might show someone she is listening, make sure to identify the different behaviors that you observed. Refer to the box "Listening." Reiterate the concept in box.

Listening

- Face the person.
- Make eye contact.
- Think about what the other person is saying.

Discuss:

Listening has two parts. First you have to pay attention to the words and then you have to let the speaker know that you have heard and understood what he or she is saying by verbally or physically acknowledging the speaker's words.

Ask:

How do you let the person know you heard him or her?

Write down what the child says, using prompts as needed. You can demonstrate listening while nodding your head and ask the child, "What did I do?"

2.2 Listening Mistakes

Engage the child by demonstrating the wrong way to listen. As you exaggerate being bored, ask:

Am I showing you I'm interested in what you are saying?

How do you know?

Write down the negative behaviors he mentions that demonstrate lack of interest or failure to listen:

- Looking away
- Leaning away from the speaker
- Grimacing and making faces
- Rolling your eyes
- Looking down
- Backing up

Switch and ask the child to be the listener. Ask him to make as many mistakes as possible while he is listening. Make sure the child interrupts, looks away, or changes the subject. When you have completed this exercise, ask:

What did you do wrong?

Write down what the child says. Make sure you include all the elements in the list.

There is another way children fail to show interest. It involves what they say or fail to say to the person who is speaking. If children have trouble identifying these behaviors, demonstrate listening the wrong way.

Write down what the child or children say.

> ### A Poor Listener
>
> - Changes the topic
> - Talks about himself or herself
> - Says nothing
> - Interrupts
> - Talks without letting the other person say anything

2.3   The Body Language of Listening

We listen with our bodies as well as our ears. When we are really interested in what someone is saying, we tend to lean toward the speaker, make eye contact, and nod in agreement. We mostly do this unconsciously, but many children with attention problems unintentionally skip all these steps, giving the listener the impression that they are not interested in the conversation.

Say:

Show me how you show someone you are listening to him.

Write down what the child says and if necessary demonstrate by pointing to your eyes and nodding. The list should include

- Mimicking the facial expressions of the speaker
- Making eye contact
- Nodding your head to indicate that you agree with the speaker or shaking your head from side to side if you disagree

The Right Way to Listen

STOP! Pay attention to the speaker.

LOOK at the speaker — make eye contact.

LEAN FORWARD slightly toward the speaker.

THINK about what the speaker is saying.

Active Listening (Nonverbal Ways of Attending):

- Nod your head in agreement or disagreement.
- Make acknowledging sounds, such as "Uh huh."

2.4 Elements of a Good Conversation: Listening and Responding

Say:

We have talked about how to listen the wrong way and how we show people we are interested using our eyes or by nodding our heads as they talk. We also use words. We ask questions, we make comments, we give compliments, and we make statements.

These are the steps we use to have a good conversation:

- We listen and try to understand the meaning of the words.
- We respond by using appropriate body language — for example, we make eye contact and nod.
- We verbally ask questions and make comments.
- We speak in short phrases so that the conversation goes back and forth like a Ping-Pong ball.

Active Listening: Verbal Ways of Responding

- Ask questions: "I don't get what you mean. Will you explain it?"
- Paraphrase or restate: "You said you liked the film because it was scary."
- Make comments: "I see what you mean."
- State facts: "The Rams won last night. It was a close game."
- Give compliments: "That's really cool."
- Make guttural sounds: "Uh huh," "umm," and so on.

2.5   Different Types of Questions

Ask:

Why do we ask questions?

We ask questions to try to get more information—for example, "I don't get what you mean, will you explain it?"

Asking questions is a really good way to let someone know that you are following and are interested in what he or she is saying. Asking questions also is a great way to get more information about what your friend thinks, feels, or likes to do. A good story always answers the following questions: Who? Why? What? When? Where? You can use all of these to ask for more information.

Open-ended questions are very useful because they open up the conversation by asking for more information. They cannot be answered simply. When you give the compliment "What a cool model" and then ask the question "How did you make it?" the answer will probably include details of how the person made the model. Likewise, if you ask "Why did you decide to make a model of this ship?" the answer will include a lot of information about the person.

Open-Ended Questions

Open-ended questions start with

Who?

What? "What was the movie about?"

Why? "Why did you think it was scary?"

When?

Where?

Closed-ended questions have simple one-word answers, such as yes or no, or they can be answered with a simple phrase.

Closed-Ended Questions

Closed-ended questions have a single answer, such as yes or no.

Person 1: What's your name?

Person 2: John.

Person 1: When did school start?

Person 2: At 8 o'clock.

Person 1: *(thinks to himself, "Now what do I say? This guy is real hard to talk to!)"*

Ask the child to give you an example of an open-ended and a closed-ended question.

Paraphrasing questions show the speaker that we heard his or her words but aren't sure about the meaning. Paraphrasing can also be a way of asking for more information.

Example: *What did you mean when you said, "I hate school"?*

2.6   Other Kinds of Responses

Discuss some of the other ways that we respond to people. Again, the child may recognize most of these conversational responses but may lack the knowledge of how to categorize them.

Lead this discussion by giving examples.

Comments. One good way to show interest is to make a comment about what the person said. "Yeah, I liked the ending. It was scary."

Restating. Another good way to show interest is to restate what the person said. "So, you liked how the movie ended?"

Statements. Statements add facts or opinions to what the person has said. "I liked the part in the movie where he told her about the hidden treasure."

Compliments. Using compliments lets the other person know that you appreciate him or her, whether your comment is a simple "Gee, that's cool" or a more detailed "I love it when you tell that story. You make it seem so real."

Guttural sounds. Responsive sounds don't add content, but they let the person know that you are following him or her. They are considered to be encouraging sounds, like "Uh huh" and "hmm."

2.7   How to Deal with Perseveration

Conversations are supposed to be an exchange between people. One person talks, and the other listens, nods, adds a comment, or asks a question. Conversations enable people to share how they think or feel about the topic at hand. Both people are supposed to take turns. Some children with SN just start talking and keep on going. They don't even stop long enough to let the other person make a comment. When these children perseverate, it is as though they are stuck on a track or on a detail and can't seem to stop. They talk way past the point of the listener's interest and may not seem to notice or even care. They break the rule that a conversation is supposed to be an exchange of information. Say:

Conversations are exchanges. You are supposed to share the airtime. Think of a conversation as a Ping-Pong ball. You keep batting the ball over the net. Try to make your conversation go back and forth like the ball.

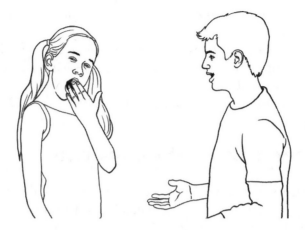

★ To illustrate this, play the "Blah Blah" game.

Start a nonsensical conversation with the child in which she can only use a nonsense phrase like "blah blah." Illustrate asking a question, such as "Blah blah blah?" Ask the child to respond to you using something like "Uh, blah blah blah blah." Change the intonation, volume, and pace to illustrate excitement, anger, and happiness.

Ask the child to notice how fast the conversation goes back and forth.

Ask the child to identify the content by the tone, volume, and pace.

★ Another game that can be used to illustrate how the conversation should go back and forth is "Hot Potato." This is a group game.

Have the children stand in a circle. Throw a ball to a child. The child who catches the ball needs to say something and throw the ball to someone else. Only the person who has the ball can talk. At the end of the game, hold on to the ball and refuse to throw it to anyone else.

Ask the children:

How does it feel when I hold the ball and refuse to throw it to anyone else? Do you think to yourself, "She doesn't want to play with me anymore?" When you talk and don't share the conversation, do you think that people think the same thing? How do children react when you do 90 percent of the talking?

Discuss the topic of how children react when you talk too much (see box).

How Children React When You Talk Too Much

- Pretend to be interested
- Change the subject
- Get mad
- Walk away
- Tease you to get you to stop
- Tell you to stop
- Hit or shove you
- Make fun of you
- Interrupt

Most children lose interest if they are not engaged in a back-and-forth exchange. If the child is polite, he or she will wait for a chance to ask a question or change the topic. Sometimes he will simply walk away. No matter how the child responds, the experience he remembers is of being bombarded by too much talking, which leaves him wanting to avoid the child who talks too much.

2.8   Arranging a STOP Sign

Say:

Sometimes I get lost when you talk too long or talk about a subject that I'm not interested in. Since we are supposed to take turns, if I am not following you or if I want to change the subject, I am going to give you a sign. When I give you this sign, it means that I want you to take ten seconds to finish up. Finishing can mean that you conclude the topic, ask me if there is something else I would rather talk about, or just be quiet and listen. The sign means you need to STOP and change what you're doing.

Arrange a **STOP** signal that you will give the child if you can't follow him or her after forty-five seconds or if this isn't a good time for you to listen to the child.

Say:

When you see the STOP signal, take ten seconds and change your course of action. Do one of these things:

- *Stop talking*
- *Ask a question like*

  "Are you interested in this?"

  "What would you like to talk about?"

  "Is this a bad time to talk?"

  "Am I talking too much?"

When you give the child the prearranged signal (such as making a "T" with your hands), she needs to stop and change what she is doing. When a child gets a STOP sign, she needs to stop and think about the other person. Instruct her to take a few deep breaths, focus on what she was trying to say, and draw it to a conclusion in one or two sentences.

Discuss the various responses with the child about alternative behavior, referring to the box "Stop and Switch Roles."

Stop and Switch Roles

1. **STOP.** Prompt the child to stop talking and to switch roles and be the listener by asking a question.
2. **Ask.** Prompt the child to check, **"Is this a bad time to talk?"**

(continued)

(continued)

3. **Make a comment.** Suggest that the child say, "I guess I'm boring you with all these facts." Prompt him to follow his statement with a question — for example, "So, how did you like your new computer game?"
4. **Conclude and ask a redirecting question.** Prompt the child to say, "I guess that sums it up. So, what did you do this weekend?"

★ Every time a child stops when you give him a signal, give him a star on his behavior sheet, a chip if you are using a behavioral reward system, or a compliment. If this is one of the child's target behaviors, you can use Exercise 12.

Exercise 9: Listening Facts

Here are some things to think about when you listen:

- What is the speaker saying?
- Do I understand what he or she means?
- Do the person's words and his or her body language agree?
- How do I show that I am interested?

In this picture, is the boy who is listening showing that he is interested or bored?

Is the boy listening and interested? How can you tell?

Exercise 10: Eye Contact

Why is it important to have good eye contact?

Do people think you are listening if you don't look at them?

Is this true in all cultures?

Give two examples of times you can't have good eye contact.

1. _____

_____

_____

2. _____

_____

_____

Socially ADDept

Exercise 11: It's Those Eyes!

James avoids eye contact with everyone. He looks away when someone is talking to him.

How does it feel to talk to James?

Nancy stares when she talks.

How do you feel when someone stares at you?

Leslie makes you feel good when she looks at you. She looks as she listens, and her eyes show you she is interested.

How does it feel to talk to Leslie?

Exercise 12: Stopping When Asked

Week of: _____

Not stopping when asked to do so is very annoying to others. Ask the child to evaluate what she did when she was asked to stop. Spend a week or two asking the child to record whether she stopped when asked and to think of what she did instead.

I stopped talking when _____

Instead, I

_____

    Asked if they were bored

    Asked if they wanted to talk about something different

    Said nothing and just hung out together being quiet

_____

_____

_____

_____

_____

_____

Verbal Conversational Skills

People listen and respond both verbally and nonverbally to what another person says through their words and their actions, showing their interest through their nonverbal use of eye contact, gestures, and body posture. The previous lessons discussed how to listen and how to ask questions; in this lesson, we discuss the two parts to a conversation, the four types of friendships, and with whom we should discuss private facts of feelings.

Ask: *What are two parts of a conversation?*

Answer: Listening and responding

Ask: *How much time do we spend listening?*

Answer: 55 percent

Ask: *What happens if we do all the talking?*

Answer: The other person gets bored and thinks we do not care about him or her.

In this lesson, we discuss the skills of how to exchange greetings and how to start, continue, and end a conversation.

3.1 Greetings

Ask: *How do you greet someone when you see him or her for the first time that day?*

Answers: Greetings can be formal and involve a handshake and a "Nice to meet you" or even "How do you do?," or they can be more informal, such as smiling and saying, "Hi." All greetings include a smile or a nod to acknowledge that you see the other person.

> "Hey, what's up?"
>
> "Hey, how's it going?"
>
> "How're you doing?"

Ask:

> *Do boys in your school use any elaborate handshakes as a way of saying "Hi"? What do their greetings look like?*

Have the child demonstrate how he has observed boys greeting each other.

Share the following information:

> *Handshakes are often used in more formal situations, but many boys use a variation of a handshake or a "knuckle bump" to indicate their special friendship. These handshakes have many variations that are unique to different male friendship groups. In formal situations, girls also shake hands as a greeting. Children sometimes greet adults with a handshake when they are being introduced for the first time.*
>
> *Hugging can be used as a greeting, although it is usually reserved for close friends and relatives. In some cultural subgroups, men and women greet each other by hugging or by kissing each other on the cheek. They may also walk down the street arm in arm or holding hands. In our culture, this is viewed as intimate contact.*

Because hugging or kissing the wrong person is awkward for everyone, advise the child only to hug or kiss people who come to his or her house. In other words, reserve it for relatives and close family friends.

Ask:

> *How do you greet the same person the second or third time you see him or her in the same day? Do you greet the person the same way?*

After the child answers, discuss this topic.

> *You don't greet the person the same way the second or third time you see him or her (at the same event or on the same day). The second time you see the person, you acknowledge him or her with a nod or a minor verbal greeting, such as "Hey" or "Hi" or a smile. The third time you see the person, a nod or a smile is enough.*

3.2   Conversation Openers: Small Talk

Discuss these ideas with the child:

> *Conversations have a sequence. They start with a verbal or nonverbal greeting, which is followed by a conversation opener (often referred to as small talk).*
>
> *The purpose of small talk is to exchange pleasantries and, often, to check out if you and the other person have anything in common. The most common openers are comments about shared experiences.*

Discuss the box "The Purpose of Small Talk." Probe to find out what the child knows about small talk. Does he know what it is or why he should bother doing it?

The Purpose of Small Talk

- To get to know the person
- To identify any shared interests
- To see if you both want to get to know each other better

Discuss the function of small talk with the child:

Small talk functions as an "icebreaker." Its purpose is to acknowledge the other person and to figure out if you both have anything in common. Frequently, people make statements about what they think they may have in common, or they say such pleasantries as "What a nice day." These short exchanges are supposed to be lighthearted.

Some possible topics include making short comments about a shared experience, such as the weather, a current event, or something that you recently saw on television or on the Internet. Sometimes men comment on a favorite team that just won or lost a specific game. Some people ask questions, such as "Did you hear that there was a fire in . . . ?" Others might open with compliment, such as "I love your dress; where did you get it?"

But many people skip small talk because they think it isn't important and they don't see how it adds to the conversation.

Ask the child to demonstrate small talk.

Pretend to greet someone for the first time.

You may have to give examples of topics that the child can use. Refer to the box "Topics for Small Talk."

Topics for Small Talk

Weather: "Gee, it's been hot."

Local current events: "Did you hear that the fire . . . ?"

A question about a popular sports team: "Did you see the . . . game?"

A comment about a popular TV show, computer game, or movie: "I really like the show *America's Got Talent*. Did you see it last night?"

A compliments on the other person's attire (clothes or accessories): "I love your . . . ; where did you get it?"

3.3 The Middle of the Conversation: Asking Questions and Making Comments

Discuss the types of remarks or questions that extend the conversation.

The middle of the conversation involves exchanging information, facts, opinions, or feelings. Sometimes the middle of a conversation includes jokes. In most cases, one person shares some information about himself or makes a comment on something that affects both people, and then the other person asks a question, makes a statement, offers an opinion, or shares information about herself as well. For instance, in the middle of a conversation, you might share something about yourself and then ask a question. "I like playing soccer after school. Do you play soccer?" If the answer is no, you could follow the response with another question: "What do you like to do after school?"

To expand the conversation, you need to figure out what the person's interests are, and this is done by asking questions that show him that you are interested in what he has to say. About 80 percent of initial conversations consist of asking questions so you can establish what interests you have in common, if any.

Review open- and closed-ended questions:

Remember when we talked about open-ended and closed-ended questions? Asking open-ended questions is the better way to find out more information about a person.

Demonstrate greeting someone and asking closed-ended questions. For example, ask: "How's it going? Have you been here long?"

Ask the child:

Do you see that you have to figure out what to say next when you used closed-ended questions (that have yes or no answers)?

Practice asking open-ended questions with children, reminding them that open-ended questions literally open up the conversation. This is a good group or class-room activity. The following box, "What Do You Like to Do: How to Use Both Open- and Closed-Ended Questions" illustrates how to start a conversation with a closed-ended question and then shift to asking open-ended questions.

"What Do You Like to Do?" How to Use Both Open- and Closed-Ended Questions

Open-ended questions are in italics.

What do you like to do on the weekend? (yes-or-no answer)
What do you like about doing . . . ? Why do you like it?

Have you played *Rock Band* [or name some other current computer game]? (yes-or-no answer)
What level did you get to? (closed-ended)

How did you do that?

What kind of music do you listen to? (closed-ended)

When did you get into ...? (can be closed- or open-ended)

What do you like about it?

Who's your favorite singer? (closed-ended)

What's your favorite song? (closed-ended)

What do you like about the singer?

Do you have a special pet? (closed-ended)

Why did your family choose a big dog? How do you take care of him?

What do you like to do with your friends? (can be closed- or open-ended)

What do you like to do when you're alone? (closed-ended)

When did you get into _____ [activity]? Why do you like it?

Remind the children to continue to use active listening body language as they listen to the answers to their questions or comments.

Active Listening: How to Show Interest Nonverbally

Nod head in agreement or disagreement.

Make encouraging guttural sounds, such as "Uh huh" and "Hmm."

Say:

Once you have established that you have a common interest, you usually talk about that sport, musical group, or game by asking questions, agreeing with the other person, disagreeing, offering facts, making comments or jokes—always making sure that you listen as much as you talk.

Ask a child to help you demonstrate how you can use questions to keep the focus on the child and what interests him or her:

What's your favorite TV show?

(Child answers.)

Did you see it last night?

(Child answers.)

What do you think is going to happen in the next episode?

(Child answers.)

You make a comment: *Those dudes are weird. Have you ever met people like that?*

After the demonstration, discuss:

A good conversation goes back and forth between the two speakers. If you are talking for more than one or two minutes without getting feedback from the other person, you are not sharing the airtime. The person will get bored or annoyed. Often, it is the lack of sharing that makes the other person want to leave.

3.4   Other Ways to Continue a Conversation

Discuss some other types of exchanges and how they also elicit more information or add information to the conversation. Refer to the box "Other Ways to Continue a Conversation."

Other Ways to Continue a Conversation

Ask questions	Leads to more information: who, what, when, how, why.
Make encouraging comments	Conveys interest. "I liked that you . . . "
Ask clarifying questions	Gets more information. "Can you tell me more? I don't get what you mean."
Paraphrasing what was said to verify if you understood it correctly	Shows you are listening, understanding, or verifying meaning. "So you said that you liked Jennifer better than Alice. Is that what you meant? Did something happen?"
Summarizing statements	Reviews or pulls ideas together. "So after you compared them all, you liked the first one best."
Compliments	Acknowledges something positive that you like about the person. "I love your . . . "

3.5   Exiting a Conversation

Discuss the importance of paying attention to negative or unfriendly body language as a way of gauging the other person's interest. Children are supposed to see unfriendly body language as a cue to end the conversation.

We have discussed that it is important to pay attention to how the other person responds to you.

Ask:

If he doesn't seem friendly, do you keep on trying to talk to him?

How can you tell if he wants to keep talking?

Did you observe his body language? Did he smile? Or did he look away?

Remind the child:

> *You are supposed to continually evaluate the other person's interest as the conversation proceeds. If the person does not seem to warm up to you (meaning that she answers in short phrases, avoids eye contact, or uses a gruff, bothered tone), you should process this as a cue to end the conversation.*

Say:

> *When you want to end a conversation, there are a number of polite ways to say good-bye. The most common phrase is "I have to go; I'll see you later." If you are sitting down, you stand up (indicating that the talk is over) and offer to shake hands, wave, or nod while saying something like "Nice talking with you."*
>
> *Many people says things like "I'll call you later" or "Let's get together sometime." This is often a throwaway line that can confuse you because the person doesn't usually mean the words literally. Often the other person has no intention of calling you or getting together later. So why do people use these expressions?*

Answer: They are considered to be polite ways of exiting a conversation.

Ask the child for other polite phrases that someone could use to say good-bye that shouldn't be taken literally.

Discuss how to tell if the person's words match her affect or their actions. If they don't match, the person is probably being polite.

> Questions to ask:
>
> *Does the person actually call you later?*
>
> *What did the person's body language say? Was it distracted, angry bored, or uninterested?*

> ★ Practice polite ways of saying good-bye with the child. The methods should be both direct and indirect.
>
> *"Excuse me, I have to go now" or "I have to leave now; I just got a phone call I have to take."*

3.6   Conversation Mistakes

A common mistake that children make is to respond by switching the topic (away from what the speaker was discussing), so that they end up talking about themselves, sharing personal information or their own experiences or opinions that may or may not be related to what the other person was talking about.

Ask and discuss:

> *What happens when you say nothing and don't ask questions?*
>
> *What happens when you just talk about yourself?*
>
> *How does it feel when someone talks without listening to you?*
>
> *How do you feel when someone doesn't listen to you?*
>
> *Do you like the person? Do you want to spend more time with him or her?*
>
> *Or do you go find another friend who shows that she cares about you?*

> *If you only talk about yourself or your interests, other children will avoid you.*

Review and discuss all the elements in the box "Mistakes That Ruin Friendships." Ask the child to give examples of each type of mistake.

Mistakes That Ruin Conversations

- Only talking about yourself
- Failing to observe the listener's interest by reading his or her body language
- Changing the subject to what you are interested in
- Not showing interest when someone else is talking
- Interrupting a conversation between two people
- Sharing personal feelings with someone you just met
- Ignoring STOP signs when the other person looks bored or annoyed or shows discomfort

3.7   The Four Kinds of Friendship and When to Share Feelings

Introduce the topic:

There are four different types of friendships, and we share different things with each group. If you make a mistake and share too much information with a casual acquaintance, the person is often uncomfortable. It is appropriate to share your feelings with a good friend or with your family. You don't tell strangers too much personal information about you or your family. Can you give me an example of someone telling you something that made you uncomfortable?

Discuss the box "Four Kinds of Friendship."

Four Kinds of Friendship

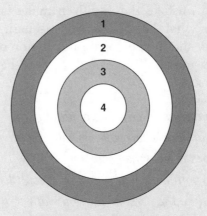

1. Strangers or new acquaintances — share facts, ask questions
2. Casual acquaintances (children you meet or share a class with at school but with whom you rarely speak) — share facts, ask questions, offer opinions, and joke

3. Associational friends (children with whom you may share an after-school activity, who seem friendly but never extend invitations to you to get together) — share opinions, share jokes, share information about your likes or dislikes
4. Really close friends and family (people who you see on an ongoing basis at home and who show you they care about you through actions, words, and deeds) — share feelings and private details of your life

Remember: Do not share personal information or feelings with people in circles 1, 2, or 3.

Say:

> *When you meet someone for the first time, there is no reason that he or she should care about how you feel. Therefore, do not share personal information or your feelings with strangers or casual acquaintances.*

Social Rule: Don't talk about your feelings with someone you don't know well — feelings are for family and close friends.

> *The difference between an acquaintance and a friend is tricky for many children and adults. Associational acquaintances are people you like and with whom you can tell a joke or talk to at school or during a common after-school or outside activity. Friends are people that you get together with after school or on weekends, or people you talk to after school, whether online or on the telephone. Friends become close through spending time together, through sharing personal information, and through showing caring and concern for each other. It is appropriate to share feelings with close friends, but not with people you barely know. Before sharing feelings, try to think to yourself, "Why would this person care?"*

3.8   Off-Limits Topics

Discuss off-limits topics:

> *There are some topics that can be very offensive to people who are different from you (different race, religion, or socioeconomic class). Comments or jokes that are generalizations about the characteristics or mannerisms of these groups are also often offensive to someone who identifies with the group.*

Children need to learn that pointing out how someone is different and making generalizations about someone's race, religious, or ethnic group are off-limit topics for conversation and jokes.

Although comedians often tell jokes using off-limit topics, they are very skilled at reading their audiences' reactions and are quick to change their dialogue to distract those who are offended. Children may miss that their audience isn't laughing or that listeners are responding with disgusted looks. If there is an awkward silence, it probably means that the child has offended someone and needs to stop and apologize.

> **Off-limit topics include comments about race, religion, ethnicity, politics, or financial status, or any comments about someone who has a physical or mental characteristic that makes him or her different.**

Discuss how girls often do not tell another girl that what she said or did was hurtful or unacceptable. Instead, they often passively express their anger or disapproval through gossip.

Teacher or parent note: If you are working with a girl, you might want to discuss how gossip works. Because gossip is also one of the ways that girls get close to each other, it might be hard for her to know when gossip is appropriate and when it isn't. You might have to role-play some situations to help her see how she would feel if she were the subject of negative gossip or a rumor. (For a more complete discussion of gossiping and rumors, see Simmons, 2002, and Wiseman, 2002.)

★ Exercises 13 through 15 are good, classroom listening games. Exercise 16 is a parent-child activity.

Exercise 13: Sharing the Airtime

This game requires a group of two or more children, or you can be a player with a single child. For children who perseverate, use a timer and a ball. When the timer (set for thirty to forty-five seconds) goes off, have the child throw the ball to you or another child. Whoever catches the ball has to make a comment about what the last person said, ask a question, or introduce a new topic and then throw the ball to someone else, who then gets to talk.

Exercise 14: Listening and Adding to the Story

A favorite group game is a variation of Telephone. The leader starts a story, creating the characters and plot, and after a minute or two (use a timer), asks another child to continue the story. After one to two minutes, the speaking role moves to the next child, who picks up the story and adds to it. This is a good way to practice listening to each other.

Exercise 15: TV Host

The purpose of this exercise is to practice greeting someone, making him or her feel comfortable, and starting and continuing a conversation.

One child plays the role of TV host and another child is the guest. The role of the TV host is to greet the guest, make him or her feel comfortable, and get the guest to talk about topics that interest him or her.

Set a timer for two minutes to allow the host to make up questions for the speaker. Remind him or her of the question words: Who? What? Where? Who? How? When?

Exercise 16: Using the Telephone (for Children at Home)

Children need to learn how to use the telephone to make connections and to set up future dates.

Arrange for your child to call up someone he or she knows to practice asking open-ended questions. If your child doesn't know whom to call, arrange with a family friend or cousin to accept the telephone call. Your child needs to identify who he or she is and to have an identified reason for making the call, such as wanting to continue a conversation, find out some specific information about a school assignment, or set up a play date. See if your child can use the conversation to find out at least two new things about the other person.

If possible, try to listen to the conversation to see if your child is practicing listening, giving compliments, and asking questions. The purpose of this exercise is for the child to become familiar with using the phone to extend invitations and to continue making connections with other children.

Exercise 17: How Do Boys Greet Each Other at Your School? How Do Girls Greet Each Other?

Observe how boys at your school use handshakes to say "Hi." Do they use "high fives," "knuckle bumps," or some other variation of a handshake when they greet each other for the first time that day? Do certain groups of boys greet each other differently?

Draw a picture of how the boys said "Hi" to each other.

Observe how girls at your school greet each other, and draw a picture of what you saw.

Exercise 18: How Do Children Say Good-Bye to Each Other?

Observe children playing, and notice how they say good-bye when the bell rings. Do boys and girls say good-bye the same way? Write down what they said.

_____

_____

_____

_____

_____

_____

_____

_____

_____

_____

_____

_____

_____

_____

_____

_____

_____

_____

_____

_____

Communicating Feelings Through Body Language

This lesson focuses on how children use body language and space to communicate their feelings to one another. Most people unconsciously reflect back to the person speaking, using similar gestures or echoing with a similar tone. This is often so subtle that it eludes the children with SN, who have specific problems comprehending and copying body language and tone. They don't participate in this feedback loop and are often unaware that it occurs. This lesson suggests some specific rules to orient children as to how people use body language to communicate their feelings and how children can learn to mimic the gestures and tone of others to appear as if they are "in sync" even if they are not. (However, the act of mimicking may have the side effect of improving their rapport. One of the tricks that therapists learn when they want to connect with a difficult client is to copy the client's body language, facial expressions, and gestures, which often causes the person to feel more connected to the therapist.)

Discuss the following information with the child.

Nonverbal signals and gestures make up over 60 percent of any communication. People use their facial expressions and gestures to communicate their feelings, mood, or interest (or lack thereof). One of the most reliable ways to understand the meaning of what a person is saying is to be able to "read" his or her body language. Many children with SN are so intent on comprehending the verbal message (the spoken words) that they often miss the emotional message conveyed in the body language and tone. Many communications do not make sense if you don't comprehend the emotional "meta-message," as this is the level that cues the listener as to whether this is a joke, a friendly statement, a hostile message, and so on. When children fail to understand the meta-message, it creates a profound weakness because they really don't know the difference between what someone says and what he or she may intend. Children who are weak in this area will need to spend more time on this section to ensure that they can track the emotional message being conveyed by body language and tone.

Discuss some of the mistakes that people make with their body language (see box) and probe to see if the child knows why these are mistakes.

Body Language Mistakes

1. Violating a person's personal space
2. Using too loud or harsh a tone when you speak
3. Failing to make eye contact
4. Grimacing or rolling your eyes
5. Touching someone too much or too intimately
6. Backing away
7. Not stopping when asked to do so

4.1   Facial Expressions

Say:

One way we let someone know that we understand his or her emotional state is to respond to what he or she said by adopting similar facial expressions as well as body gestures and tone. Girls often reflect each other's feelings, often without knowing they have done it, by mimicking the other girl's body language and tone. You can create a sense of closeness by intentionally copying or reflecting a person's body language and tone.

Ask: *Why is it important to know how someone is feeling?*

Answers:

- To respond to the person correctly
- To judge interest
- To understand if the person is serious or joking
- To judge if this is a good time to approach
- To share feelings and feel close
- To understand if the person is annoyed and wants you to stop

4.2   It's Those Eyes

Say:

Someone's eyes can tell you a lot about how a person feels. When a person wants to make contact with you, he will raise his eyebrows, which makes his eyes appear larger and more penetrating. Conversely, if he isn't interested, he may avoid eye contact entirely, and his posture might sag slightly. In some cultures, people believe that the eyes are the window to a person's soul. What does that mean? Can you tell how someone is feeling from the look in her eyes?

Discuss these ideas:

- If someone is friendly, he or she will look directly at you.
- If someone is bored or wants to avoid you, he or she will look away from you.
- If someone is making fun of you or is annoyed with you, he or she often rolls his or her eyes upward and makes a face, or purses his or her lips.
- When someone is lying, he or she often cannot maintain eye contact (using an intermittent darting gaze).
- When someone is embarrassed or ashamed, he or she often avoids eye contact.

Demonstrate the importance of facial expressions by saying "I'm so happy" while frowning and looking at the floor.

Ask: *Did you believe I was happy?*

A person's eyes, the expression on her face, her gestures, her posture—all reflect how a person feels. We use them to understand what a person's words mean (particularly if the words and the body language message disagree, which we'll talk about in a later lesson).

Discuss the body language checklist (see box).

Nonverbal Communication: The Body Language Checklist

1. Is the expression in the person's eyes friendly or unfriendly?
2. What about eye contact? Does the person look directly at you, look away, look down, or look at you with a "darting glance"?
3. Is the person's body posture open or closed?
4. Is the person's facial expression happy, sad, angry, annoyed, or frightened?
5. What do the person's posture and gestures say? Is he open or closed? Are the gestures small and weak or animated and big? Do you think the person is being serious or playful?
6. How close does the person stand to you? Does she seem as though she is trying to get away, or conversely, is she too close?
7. Is the person leaning toward you or away from you? Is he standing up straight or slouching away?
8. Does the person talk in a mean tone? Does she sound annoyed or angry?

★ A good classroom or group activity is to practice reading facial expressions by playing Feeling Charades. The teacher or group leader either uses an commercial deck of "feeling cards" or gathers photographs of children and has the children cut and paste the pictures onto feeling cards that they label themselves. (For children who need more help with reading feelings, making the cards themselves may help them retain the associations with the images and the feelings.) Include as many of the following feelings as possible:

Fearful	Lucky	Anxious	Relieved
Angry	Embarrassed	Frustrated	Overwhelmed
Sad	Important	Bored	Guilty
Jealous	Proud	Happy	Disgusted

A child is chosen to pick out a feeling card, such one showing a sad face, and she has to mimic the expression on the card in front of the other children. The other children have to guess which feeling she is copying. Remind the children to pay attention to her eyes, her gestures, and her posture.

Parents can do the same activity at home with the parent(s) and child (including other siblings as well). The instructions are the same.

I recommend Dr. Simon Baron-Cohen's 2009 DVD on building feeling recognition. If the child needs more practice identifying feelings, please see Lesson Five.

4.3   Open or Closed Gestures and Posture

Say:

Gestures and posture also tell us what people are feeling. Hand gestures can say lots of things.

Ask the child to demonstrate these statements by moving his hands, shoulders, and neck. (If the child happens to use facial expressions as well, that is OK. The idea here is for to see how his gestures communicate as well.)

"Back off."

"I don't know."

"What?"

Body gestures can also let us know what someone is thinking or feeling. What do these gestures mean?

Demonstrate these gestures to the child and ask what they mean:

Shrugging your shoulders

Answer: "I don't know."

Leaning toward someone

Answer: "I'm interested."

Leaning away

Answer: "I'm not comfortable."

Backing away

Answer: "I want to go."

All these gestures and postures tell us something. If someone is interested, he or she will tend to lean toward you and have open body language.

If someone is bored, disapproving, or uncomfortable, his or her body posture will be closed—for example, the person will stand with his or her arms crossed over the chest, leaning away from you and avoiding eye contact.

★ Play a game of mirroring: Simon Says, Mimic Me. The purpose of this exercise is to for children to pair up and copy the body posture, gestures, and facial expressions of the other child. Assign one child as the leader, and the other child follows and copies every gesture and expression that the leader does. Then the children reverse roles. (If you are a parent doing this at home, pair the child with a sibling, or do the exercise with your child, letting him or her copy you first.)

Give these instructions:

I want you followers to copy whatever your leader does—if he slouches in the chair, crosses his legs, looks away, pretends he is Godzilla—your job is to copy all your leader's gestures and expressions. We want the leaders to think they are looking into a mirror.

At the end of the exercise, switch roles or pair the children up with a different child. When the exercise is over, ask to followers:

When you were the mirror, copying the other child's gestures, how did you feel?
Ask the leaders:

When the child copied you, how did you feel? Did you feel any closer to the child who mirrored you?

★ Here's a simple activity for parents: At various times during the week, ask your child to identify how you are feeling by reading your body language. Are you in a hurry, harried, happy, glad, sad, relaxed, or uptight? Let your child know when he or she is right!

> **Copying body language creates unconscious rapport.**

This is an important activity because you want your child to know when you are feeling harried or stressed so that he or she can judge when to leave you alone. If your child is totally oblivious to your emotional state, ask him or her to look at you and judge whether this is a good time.
Ask your child:

How do I look? Do you think this is a good time to ask me to help you?

4.4 Respecting Personal Space

Ask the child:

Have you ever had the experience of someone whom you didn't know very well getting too close to you? What did you do?

Did you back up?

Did you feel uncomfortable?

We each have a space around us that we feel is our "personal space." The size of this personal space is different in various cultures. In the United States, people generally think of their personal space as equivalent to an arm's length or approximately two-and-a-half to three feet.

Demonstrate by putting out your arm and drawing an imaginary circle around yourself. Say:

This is my personal space. While I may let a close friend into this space, I won't like it if someone I don't know well gets too close.

Don't get too close to someone whom you don't know very well; the person may feel you are invading his space. Most people do not like feeling invaded, so it is very important to learn not to get too close to someone whom you don't know well.

Pay attention to how a person reacts when you get too close. Does the person pull away? If he does, that is a STOP sign.

When you are in a public place, like a movie theater or on a bus, and there are a bunch of empty seats, are you supposed to sit right next to someone you don't know?

Answer: *You aren't supposed to sit next to the stranger, because there are other seats available from which to choose. You are supposed to give the person his or her space.*

4.5   Touching People

Discuss touching, starting with these questions:

Does everyone likes to be touched?

Does it matter who touches you?

Like hugging, touching is very personal, and different cultures have different rules about what is acceptable. Although there are cultures where people greet each other with kisses and hugs, other cultures, such as ours, define touching as something that only close friends and family do with each other. Although it is always acceptable to shake hands or slap a friend on the back (this is a male approval sign) or touch someone on her back or her forearm, almost every other part of the body is off-limits unless you know the person very well.

Ask:

What are the acceptable, friendly ways to touch a friend of the same sex?

Answers can include the following:

Handshake

Pat on back

Brief touch of forearm

Hug (depending on the cultural subgroup)

Ask:

Do boys and girls at your school greet their friends in the same way? Do any of the girls hug to say "Hi" or "Good-bye"?

Do the boys greet each other in any special way? Do they shake hands, gesture, or do a variation of the knuckle bump?

The Touching Rule: If someone is uncomfortable being touched or hugged, respect that person and don't touch him or her.

How do your family members greet each other?

4.6   Stop Signs

Say:

We discussed STOP signs in Lesson Two, when you made an agreement with your teacher and your parent that you would try to stop when he or she gave you an agreed-on signal. Although then we were specifically discussing stopping when you are talking too much, the same principle applies here. We are going to review why stopping is so important.

Discuss stop signs again. Use this scenario:

Your mom is on the telephone, talking to your dad. You come in and without even asking yourself, "Is this a good time?" you start talking to her.

She gives you an annoyed or angry expression, like this. (Demonstrate an annoyed expression by frowning and shaking your head.)

What do her gestures tell you?

Describe what you saw and tell me what it means.

Review what children say:

Your eyes got smaller.

You didn't smile.

Your body stiffened.

You frowned.

You shook your head.

Ask:

Was this a "Come here" or "Go away" message?

Answer: Go away.

Stop Signs

1. Person looks away repeatedly.
2. Person turns away.
3. Person shakes his head.
4. Person rolls her eyes and shakes her head.
5. Person crosses his arms and glares at you.
6. Person either turns away from you or starts to back away from you.
7. Person's facial expression looks angry or agitated.
8. Person talks, but her tone sounds annoyed, or she uses sarcasm.

Ask:

What happens if you ignore STOP *signs?*

Answer: People get mad at you and then they avoid you or make fun of you.

> **If you don't pay attention when people tell you to stop, they won't want you to hang around with them.**

Exercise 19: Facial Expressions

Facial expressions can tell you how someone is feeling.

Connect the feelings with the pictures.

I'm angry.

I'm happy.

I feel OK.

I don't get it.

Exercise 20: Practice Identifying Feelings in Facial Expressions and Body Language

Note: This is a parent-child exercise.

1. Have the child collect pictures of a variety of people and put on cards or in a scrapbook.

   Have the child observe the facial expressions, body gestures, and postures, and decide which feeling goes with which picture.

Fearful	Lucky	Anxious	Relieved
Angry	Embarrassed	Frustrated	Overwhelmed
Sad	Important	Bored	Guilty
Jealous	Proud	Happy	Disgusted

2. With your child, watch sitcoms on television with the sound off and guess what the actors are saying and feeling.

Exercise 21: Body Language

For the pictures below, describe what the people are feeling and which body parts or gestures express their feeling:

Feeling: _____

Body part(s): _____

Feeling: _____

Body part(s): _____

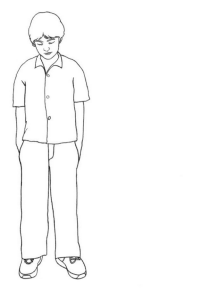

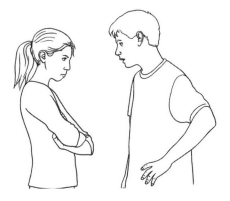

Feeling: _____

Body part(s): _____

Feeling: _____

Body part(s): _____

Exercise 22: Physical Proximity

When you get too close to people, they feel uncomfortable. Every culture has a different notion of what feels too close.

What do you think too close is in our culture?

Answer: Less than about an arm's length away

What is wrong in this picture?

Draw a picture so that both children are comfortable. How far away from each other would they be?

Being "in Sync"—Understanding and Echoing Tone

I've learned that people forget what you said, people will forget what you did, but people will never forget how you made them feel.
—Maya Angelou, talking to Oprah Winfrey on her seventieth birthday

This lesson is for those children who are weaker in understanding the meaning of tone, as is often true for children with Asperger's Syndrome and NLD. Although many programs have used visual aids to teach children how to read body language and even to mirror what they see, few programs address how to decode the emotional meta-message that is conveyed in the person's tone. This message can alter the meaning of the words.

Musical terms are often used to describe relationships when they are going well; people say "We're in harmony" or "We're in sync." Likewise, when someone is "offbeat," it means he isn't connecting well with others. Because the tone conveys the emotional part of the message, in this lesson, we describe feelings in terms of their physics, their wave form, intensity, variability, and frequency which all convey subtle differences that people respond to often unconsciously. Last, if children learn to echo the tone, it will undoubtedly increase their rapport with others.

Discuss the idea that the tone carries the emotional message and can modify the meaning of the words.

Ask:

Can you show me how your tone can show your mood or your feelings?

If necessary, you can demonstrate by saying "I really like you" while using a loud, harsh, hostile sound.

Ask:

Which comes through louder and clearer?

Answer: The tone

Consider another example.

A friend's mother dies. You know he feels bad. When you call him, you use a happy, upbeat tone. Do you think he gets the message that you understand how sad he is?

Answer: Probably not

Discuss these ideas:

Most of us create rapport (or lack thereof) unconsciously, because we are often unaware of our tone. But we can consciously create rapport by mimicking the other person's gestures and tone. If we reflect the person's emotional state back to him by using similar facial expression and tone, the person usually get the message that we understand how he feels. Echoing the tone literally puts you both on the same frequency, and the other person often feels that you "get" what he feels.

This is a skill that women often use in "rapport talk." Even if a woman doesn't understand why you feel what you do, she will often reflect your tone. It may be that in the act of sounding like you, she may actually understand you better as well.

5.1   Using Music to Teach Emotional Harmony

Many children with LD have auditory processing problems. They might find it difficult to mimic tone. They can benefit from learning to sing or play a musical instrument. A secondary benefit of learning music is that it can provide a way to socialize for children who find unstructured social events awkward. The criteria for participating in a music group is straightforward: you need to stay on the beat, to play the right note with some regularity, and to be quiet when asked to do so.

Some musical concepts that teach good communication skills that can be learned from playing in musical groups (orchestra, bands, choirs) are

- Sharing the auditory space (playing together versus soloing)
- Learning to control your volume
- Learning to blend in and harmonize
- Keeping the same rhythm

- Learning to take turns
- Learning that a soloist always comes back to the main part of the piece (checks back in with the group)
- Learning auditory discrimination of tones (frequency, intensity, volume)

Musical Concepts That Use Good Social Skills

- Sharing the auditory space — soloing versus taking turns
- Staying in rhythm — keeping on topic or theme
- Sharing the same rhythm and pattern of the notes — responding to others
- When soloing, remembering to return to the dominant pattern that the group shares
- Controlling volume — not dominating or drowning out others
- Harmonizing (staying on topic)

5.2   The Tone of Emotions

Along with mirroring someone's body language, when a child communicates well with another, he will modulate or change his tone to be closer to his friend's tone.

Discuss discord between the tones and the words:

Demonstrate saying "I'm sorry that your dad died."

First say it while imagining feeling sad and using a tone that is in a deeper register, that is slow and sounds thoughtful or serious.

Illustrate the difference when you say the same phrase, but now use a high-pitched, fast-paced tone that you might use to express happiness or joy.

Discuss the difference. Does the child hear the importance of using the right tone if you want the other person to feel that you understand her? Every feeling has its own sound, and it is important to be able to use and recognize the different tones.

Variations in tone, volume, tempo, and rhythm all can change the message. Use a phrase such as "I'm happy today" and change the volume, the tempo, and then the rhythm of the phrase.

Ask:

- *When a boy is loud, what does his tone say about him?*

Answer: He wants to be noticed, or he is insecure.

- *When a girl talks in a high-pitched tone and at a really fast pace, what does her tone say?*

Answer: People think she is anxious.

- *If a boy uses a slow, staccato rhythm with no inflection (staccato refers to choppy, evenly spaced sounds), how do people think he feels?*

Answer: They might think he is depressed or disconnected from his feelings.

Ask the child to make sounds that indicate these feelings. (The words in parentheses indicate how you might describe how to make the sounds that go with the feelings.)

- Calmness (a soothing sound)
- Anger (a harsh, sharp sound, often high-pitched)
- Excitement (fast, high-pitched, with lots of variation)
- Sadness (deep and slow)
- Fear (sharp, intense, and fast, or slow)
- Anxiety (fast and high-pitched, but sharper and more constant than for excitement)

Understanding and using tone can be particularly difficult for children with Asperger's Syndrome and NLD. They may need additional help recognizing the meaning attached to these sounds, and they may also not be accustomed to using these tones to express themselves. It is important that they learn to recognize the cadence, speed, rhythm, intensity, variability, and pitch, and how others interpret it if they speak in a monotone. If children speak in a monotone, others may think they are insensitive. Because most people vary their tone depending on the message they wish to convey, when children hear a monotone, it may make them uncomfortable (Robinson, 2007; Baron-Cohen, 2009).[1]

Assign Exercise 23: The Right Tone of Voice.

5.3 When the Tone or Body Language Disagrees with the Spoken Words

When we listen, we hear the words, but often we react unconsciously to the tone (and the body language). As we have discussed, this meta-message often comes across "louder" than the words and tunes us in to the emotional state of the person speaking.
Say:

The tone of voice we use, whether angry, annoyed, or happy, tells other people how we feel. People react to our tone more than they do to our words, so we need to make sure that our tone communicates what we want it to say.

Using an exaggerated angry tone while simultaneously tightening your mouth, squinting yours eyes, and clenching your fists, tell the child,

I'm really happy today.

Ask:

Did you believe that I was happy?

The child should say no.

Ask:

Why didn't you believe me?

Write down what the child says, reminding him or her to be specific:

- You looked cross.
- You squinted your eyes into little slits.
- You clenched your fists.
- You sounded angry.
- You clenched your teeth and pursed your lips.

Ask:

How did my tone sound?
Was it friendly or unfriendly?
Was my posture inviting and friendly? Or tight and unfriendly?

Ask: *Did you pay more attention to my tone or my words?*

Say:

We have discussed how people's words can disagree with their tone and body language or their actions. When this happens, which message is supposed to the more accurate one? How are you supposed to determine the meaning when the two message disagree?

Answer: The message in the body language and tone (often expressed unconsciously) is the more reliable predictor of how the person really feels. His emotional state can often change the meaning of his words — modifying, contradicting, or agreeing with them.

> **Always listen to the nonverbal message first (actions, body language, and tone).**

Exercise 23: The Right Tone of Voice

The tone of voice that we use, whether it is an angry, annoyed, or happy tone, tells other people how we feel. People react to our tone more than they react to our words, so make sure that your tone communicates what you want it to. Ask for feedback on your tone.

Your mother tells you a friend is on the telephone. You take the phone and say "Hi." Circle the kind of tone you should use:

cheerful   **angry**   **teasing**   **bored**   **mean**   **sincere**

Your teacher asks you to sit down and get back to your schoolwork. You answer, "OK." Try saying OK in a **snotty** tone.

How will the teacher respond to you?

A friend tells you that you are cute. Try saying "Thanks" with a **friendly** tone. Now use a **bored** tone.

Which one will get you more compliments in the future?

Your dad reminds you to take out the garbage. His tone is annoyed. You should answer him in

☐   a **sarcastic** tone   ☐   a **sincere** tone

How will your dad respond if you answer him in an **angry** tone?

★ Practice using a **friendly** tone this week. ★

Exercise 24: Volume Control

Look at this picture. Think about the importance of volume.

HEY, JACK.

. . . WANT TO
COME OVER TODAY?

Have you ever been around a boy or girl who talked too loudly?

Did you want to tell him or her to be quiet?

Has anyone ever told you that you talk too loudly or too softly?

Using the right volume is important.

There are times when it's OK to be loud, as when you are rooting for your team at a baseball game or when you are applauding at a concert.

There are also times when you need to speak softly and use less volume.

When would you want to use a softer voice?

Circle which times you would want to use a soft voice:

At the library

When you are at a ball game cheering your team

At the movie theater

When you answer your teacher

When there is an emergency and you are trying to get someone to call 911

When you tell someone a secret

Exercise 25: Practice Identifying How Feelings Sound

Note: This is a parent-child exercise.

With a parent, watch sitcoms on television with the sound on and try to identify what tones the actors use to describe their feelings. Try to identify what these feelings sound like.

Fearful	Lucky	Anxious	Relieved
Angry	Embarrassed	Frustrated	Overwhelmed
Sad	Important	Bored	Guilty
Jealous	Proud	Happy	Disgusted

Exercise 26: Copy Cat: Practicing Being in Someone Else's Shoes

In the game of Copy Cat, the child intentionally copies another child, his or her parent, a character on TV, or a friend. The goal of this exercise is for the child to gain experience in predicting someone's feelings by copying that person's body language and tone.

1. Copy the person's body language, paying attention to the facial expression and whether the person seems open or closed. Try to copy the person leaning toward or away from you.
2. Copy the tone, the rhythm, and the pace of the words and guess the feeling being communicated.
3. Paraphrase what the other person said and if his or her tone agreed with what he or she said.
4. Guess the feeling.
5. Check with the person to see whether you are right.

Note for Lesson Five

1. Children who need additional help in mimicking sounds and comprehending their meaning might benefit from the DVD *Mind Reading: An Interactive Guide to Emotion,* by Dr. Simon Baron-Cohen (2009). This is an interactive computer-based program whose aim is to help children visually (and with sound) identify feelings. In one game, for example, a child's face is broken up into sixteen squares, and the goal is to recognize the feeling on the basis of as few squares as possible. Another part of the program demonstrates the sound of the feeling and shows it as a waveform that looks like a tiny oscilloscope. (It shows the variability and intensity, which correlate to modulation and volume.) When the character uses a sad tone, the child can actually see a picture of what the tone's waveform looks like. This was intended to be a remedial program for children with Asperger's Syndrome and NLD.

   Ultimate Learning: Fun with Feelings (n.d.) is a compact disc of the music and songs that Cathy Bollinger uses to help children identify emotions and their distinctive sounds. Another helpful collection of Bollinger's is *My Turn, Your Turn: Songs for Building Social Skills.*

   Rock Band, the music video game developed by Harmonix Music Systems for PlayStation 3 and Xbox 360 and for Wii, can also be useful (although the upper levels of the game may too difficult). The beginning levels can provide a simulation of playing with a rock group for up to four players. While the music plays, the children are visually prompted to play along using their controllers (choices are lead guitar, bass guitar, and drum). They are scored on (1) how well they matched the scrolling musical notes while playing their "instruments," (2) how well they matched the singer's pitch on the vocals, and (3) how well they matched the rhythm of the drumbeat. Although this is not a remedial game, it has the capacity to teach syncopation, rhythm, and tone to some children. The game maybe more appropriate for older children. *Guitar Hero* is a similar game developed by the same company.

Recognizing Friendly Behavior

People cannot refrain from communicating, or so said Gregory Bateson (1972). People constantly communicate, whether they intend to or not, through how they move their bodies and through the sounds they make. So far, the child has experienced talking without using words by varying his or her tonal sounds and has used his or her gestures and expressions to communicate feelings to others. In this lesson, the child learns to read the gestalt, the combined meta-message deciphered from the sum of how the verbal and tonal pieces go together. This combined meta-message tells the child whether the other person is friendly or unfriendly. ("Am I getting a green light or a STOP sign?")

6.1 Recognizing Friendly Behavior

Say:

> *During the last lesson, we looked at nonverbal ways people communicate with each other. We also learned that tone and body language are sometimes more honest and reliable than the verbal messages.*

Ask: *If there is a conflict between the verbal and nonverbal messages, which one should you believe?*

Answer: The nonverbal message

123

Ask: *How do people express themselves nonverbally?*
Answer: In their body language and tone
Say: *It is important to recognize and obey both verbal and nonverbal STOP signs.*

6.2 Review of STOP Signs

In section 2.8, the teacher, parent, and child should have agreed on a prearranged nonverbal reminder to the child when the adult notices that the child is annoying someone else and ignoring the other person's request to stop. In Lesson Two, the child was asked also to pay attention to his successes and to note how he was able to stop and if he substituted another behavior or just was quiet and listened. In this section, we move the discussion to how other children (and adults) tell the child to stop (talking, interrupting, being too bossy or silly) and what happens to the child if he ignore their requests.

People tell us through their body language how they feel. Our goal is to know from observing their body language whether people are feeling friendly toward us (using approachable signs) or whether they want to be left alone. We want to practice interpreting friendly behavior and paying attention to nonverbal STOP signs.

Ask: *Why is it important to know the STOP signs that people use?*
Answers:

To judge if it is a good time to approach them

To understand how they feel

To respect others' needs and wants

If you recognize STOP signs, you will know when to approach people, how to join groups, and how to show more respect for the feelings of others.

Ask: *What are some of the most common mistakes that children make?*
Discuss these with the child:

- Failing to read and react to the tone or body language
- Disregarding an annoyed or angry tone
- Disregarding a bored expression
- Disregarding sarcasm and indirect hints
- Disregarding nonverbal messages that it is not a good time to approach the other person
- Failing to stop when asked directly to do so
- Barging in without checking for friendly signs

Ask: *What happens when you don't stop?*
Answer: The other child gets angry and wants to avoid you.

6.3   Nonverbal STOP Signs

Discuss the box "Nonverbal STOP Signs" with the child.

Nonverbal STOP Signs

You are being given a STOP sign when the person . . .

- Looks away repeatedly
- Shakes his head in disbelief
- Purses her lips and shakes her head in disapproval
- Rolls her eyes, and shakes her head, and exchanges this glance with another person, who mimics the eye roll, shakes her head and maybe shrugs (The shrug says, "What can you do?")
- Crosses her arms and glares at you
- Backs up or turns away
- Narrows his eyes into a glare or penetrating gaze (lips are pursed)
- Actually gives you a shove to push you away
- Holds out her hand in the universally accepted STOP position

Reiterate what happens when you ignore STOP signs:

When you ignore unfriendly body language or facial cues to STOP, other children get annoyed, then upset, and eventually angry or disgusted (or both). The end result is that they will want to avoid you.

Discuss the use of the checklist "How to Read Nonverbal STOP Signs" (see box). This can be used as a class exercise as well.

How to Read Nonverbal STOP Signs

Look at the person you're talking to, to see if there are any of these nonverbal cues that show disapproval.

☐ Is the **expression** in the child's eyes unfriendly? Look for rolling of eyes, squinting, or narrowing of eyes into a steely gaze. Widening of eyes (lifting the eyebrows) can mean surprise, but if it is accompanied by another other gesture, such as a deep sigh or shaking of the head, it can mean disapproval, as in "I don't believe he's doing this again!"

☐ Is the **eye contact** intermittent, or is there outright avoidance? Are there glances to another child to get him or her to also observe your behavior?

(continued)

Recognizing Friendly Behavior

(continued)

☐ Is the child leaning away from you (**body posture**) or even **backing away from you**?

☐ Is the child's **facial expression** unfriendly — for example, angry, annoyed, or worried?

☐ Is the child's **gesturing** for you to go away or pushing you away? (Blocking gestures include "bookending," which is two people turning toward each other and blocking your entrance into their conversation.)

☐ Does a girl (while talking in a group with other girls) keep looking your way, pointing at you, and laughing?

If you get any of these signs, assume they are STOP signs — and STOP.

6.4 Verbal STOP Signs

Discuss:

Children can also tell you to STOP verbally. Tone of voice is important; children get louder and more forceful as their anger increases.

Ask the child to demonstrate the following examples of verbal STOP signs.

- "Knock it off!"

- "Quit it!"

- "Are you finished yet?" (sarcastic way to say STOP)

- "Shut up." (if loud and direct — a true command)

- "Big deal."

- "So what?"

- "Whatever."

All of these can escalate into name-calling or even a physical exchange if the child doesn't heed the warning and STOP.

Ask:

If people send out STOP signs, what should you do?

Answer: Stop!

Discuss why all these are correct answers.

- STOP talking or doing what you are doing that is bothering them.

- SEE if you can figure out what bothered them.

- BE QUIET and OBSERVE.

> # Correct Responses to STOP Signs
>
> STOP.
>
> Look.
>
> Pay attention to body language and words.
>
> Change your behavior.

6.5 Reading STOP Signs

Discuss:

> *We have talked about paying attention to how people tell us* verbally and nonverbally *when they want us to STOP.*
>
> *We have also discussed the importance of respecting other people and their desires. We have talked about what happens when you approach someone who wants to be left alone.*

Ask:

> *Why is it important to know how people say STOP?*

Answer: To respect what other children want

Ask:

> *Why is it important to respect what other people want?*

Answer: To protect yourself from ridicule or rejection

Say:

> *If you annoy other children, at first they'll try to correct you (often telling you to stop in words or by using sarcasm). If you persist in being annoying, other children will avoid you. However, if you persistently continue to ignore other children's boundaries, meaning that you consistently break their rules or are pushy or aggressive, the other children often move to reject you. (See Section 7.6, Refusal Versus Rejection.)*

Ask:

> *How do you feel when someone ignores what you want?*

Answers:

It makes me angry or frustrated.

It makes me sad.

If you don't pay attention or respect what others want, they will want try to avoid you.

6.6 Play Red Light, Green Light

Note: This activity can be done with one child or as group activity. When I play this game with a group, I use a large stop sign that I purchased. If you don't have one, you can make one. You can draw or paint a green light on one side and a red light and Stop on the other.

Give the child pictures or cards with different feelings pictured on them.

If the face is friendly = **green** light

If the face is unfriendly or indifferent = **red** light

Using the cards, ask the child to demonstrate each feeling while asking him or her, "Is this a red light or a green light?"

Fear

Anger

Sadness

Anxiety

Happiness

Ask the child to describe what he or she sees:

Is the person friendly or unfriendly?

If the person is unfriendly, the child should Stop.

Reiterate which feelings are saying it is OK to approach and which feelings are saying Stop.

Act out these four feelings and ask the child to identify your feeling and whether your nonverbal communication says to "come closer" or to "stop and wait."

Happy:	Relaxed muscles, easy smile, laughing
Angry:	Tight muscles, no smile, glaring
Anxious:	Tight muscles, avoiding eye contact
Friendly:	Relaxed muscles, easy smile, eye contact

Ask:

Which feelings say Approach?

Which feelings say Stop?

6.7   Using Manners to Say STOP

(When "Later" means "No," "Stop," or "I'm not interested")

This topic was discussed in Sections 4.6 and 5.3 because many children take words so literally and misinterpret a polite refusal as genuine interest. If the child understands this concept and knows how to recognize a "mannerly refusal," you can skip this section.

Discuss:

Sometimes children and adults wish to avoid directly refusing a request. They avoid a confrontation by using phrases that are thought to be a polite way of saying no. These phrases seem to indicate interest, but they are usually delivered in a more vague, polite way. Sometimes the person will avoid eye contact. Here are some examples of how someone might say "Good-bye." In most cases, it is just a polite way of saying "Good-bye."

"Let's talk about that later."

"Yeah, see you later."

"Let's get together sometime."

"That sounds interesting . . . let's talk about that later."

"We'll see . . . "

"I'll call you later . . . "

The common characteristic is that the statements are all vague. If the person were really saying that he wants to get together or talk later, he would probably follow it up with a question like "Will you be home?" or something more specific. The actions that follow are what really tell you whether or not he means what he says.

1. Does the boy follow up and do what he says he will do (call later, and so on)?

If he does not follow up his statements with an action, he is politely saying no or "Good-bye" or "I'm not interested."
Remember that actions always speak louder than words.

2. Does his body language show interest? If a person is genuinely interested, his body language usually reflects that interest. If he keeps looking at you or glancing back or smiling and waving, those gestures indicate he is interested. If the boy is hiding how he feels, he may look away, look down, turn away—all signs that show avoidance. When you see signs like these, the person does not mean what he is saying. His body language says, "I'm not really interested in you."

Here are some questions to ask to help you figure out if a person really means what she is saying:

- *Does the tone of voice match what her words say?*
- *Does she maintain eye contact or does she look away, or look nervous?*
- *Does the person seem uncomfortable?*
- *Does her tone sound animated, or lackluster or dull?*
- *Does any of her body language contradict her words?*

Exercise 27: Reading Friendly and Unfriendly Body Language

When people feel friendly toward you, they show you with their body language and facial gestures.

Circle the children who look friendly, and put an X over the children who look unfriendly.

Exercise 28: STOP Signs

Pay attention to *nonverbal and verbal* STOP signs. Circle the nonverbal and nonverbal Stop signs you saw or heard this week:

Rolled eyes
Glared at me
Looked away repeatedly
Turned away
Crossed arms and backed away
Used arm to block me
Pointed at me and laughed

"Shut up" (depending on the inflection, this can be serious or friendly, but usually it means STOP)
"Big deal."
"So what?"
"Whatever."
Polite laugh while rolling eyes
"Are you finished?"

Record any incidents that happened when others told you to STOP. What did you do differently?

When _____ told me to stop, I . . .

Stopped doing _____

Asked him what he wanted

Asked if he was serious

Ignored him

Changed the subject

Got quiet and listened

Moved to be out of the way

Exercise 29: Recognizing How Other Children Say Good-Bye

Have you ever noticed someone avoiding saying no directly? Here are the kinds of things the person might say.

"Let's talk later."
"I'll call you later."
"Yeah, see you later."
"Let's get together sometime."
"Later."
"That sounds good..."
"We'll see..."

Practice saying no, using the indirect approach.

Joining an Ongoing Group

People communicate all the time, because their body language always tells us how they feel. In this lesson, the child learns to be a detective and use her knowledge of recognizing friendly body language to determine when to approach others. If she approaches a group and hangs out on the periphery, can she tell if the children are friendly? If so, maybe the group will accept her if she asks to join their play. In this lesson, the child learns to evaluate when and how to join others who are already engaged in a game or activity.

Review what the child has learned about body language.

We have looked at the nonverbal ways that people communicate and have identified friendly versus unfriendly behaviors. People show interest in us nonverbally by

1. *Making eye contact*
2. *Smiling*
3. *Extending greetings*
4. *Making friendly gestures*
5. *Using friendly facial expressions*

The STOP signs include

1. *Avoiding eye contact*
2. *Frowning instead of smiling*

3. *Failing to acknowledge your presence (giving no verbal or nonverbal greeting)*

4. *Backing away*

Review by asking:

Why is it important to know the stop signs people use?

- *To judge if it is a good time to approach someone*
- *To understand how others are feeling*
- *To respect other people and their needs and wants*

If you recognize stop signs, you will know how to approach people, join groups, and show respect for others.

7.1 Joining a Group

Say:

Learning how to join an ongoing activity is a skill. First you approach a group slowly and you use your knowledge of body language to tell you if the children are friendly or not. Anyone can approach a group to watch their game, but you should only ask to join a game if the children playing appear to be open to you. You can judge this by making small comments, and if you don't get back any positive response and no positive, friendly body language, then the message is just to stay and watch the game or find another activity to do. You can judge the friendliness of the group by reading their body language.

Ask:

Why do you think we need to know how to join a group?

How do we judge if the children are being friendly or not?

Emphasize that children should only ask to join a group when they get a green light. If they wait for a green light, they will be

- Protecting themselves from getting hurt
- Respecting the desires of other children

7.2 Join, Don't Intrude

Many impulsive children go right up to other children who are already playing a game, and, without even watching, they jump right in and ask if they can join the game. Because they didn't take the time to check the score or to see if the game was nearly over, they are frequently refused. If the other children aren't ready to include someone new, they will say no.

The goal is to teach the child how to judge the interest of the other children, so that she can see if and when the others might accept her if she asks to join. This method protects the child from being refused and feeling rejected.

When psychologists studied how popular children join activities, they found that popular children do not barge in; they wait to be invited to play or wait until the game is over and offer to join the "losing side" or the side with fewer players.

Discuss the box "How Do Popular Children Join a Group?"

How Do Popular Children Join a Group?

- They wait.
- They watch the game.
- They join as an observer and make friendly comments or give compliments like "Nice shot!"
- They cheer on the team.
- They wait for the game to be over before asking to join.
- If they don't know how to play the game, they just watch. They do not attempt to join a game they don't know how to play.
- Boys offer to join or "help" the losing team or the one with fewer players.
- Girls make eye contact with the game's leader and address her.

Fifty percent of the time, popular children are not invited to join an ongoing game. Unlike many other children, they don't take refusal personally; instead, they either just continue to watch the game or go elsewhere to play.

7.3 Demonstrate the Wrong Way to Join a Group

NOTE: Because of the sensitive nature of this exercise, it is not a good classroom exercise. It should be done in a safe setting, such as in a small group or with a parent.

Ask:

What is the wrong way to try to join a group?

Answers can include the following:

- You barge in.
- You brag about how well you can play.
- You say negative comments to the other children if you are refused (for example, "I don't want to play your stupid game.")
- You disrupt the game.

To do this role play, you need a minimum of three children to participate. The adult's role is to be the coach (unless you don't have three children to do this exercise). Instruct two (or more) children to pretend to be playing a game of cards or a board game. Instruct the third child to be the newcomer who is going to barge in and ask to play (joining the wrong way). If the child is being too polite, whisper in her ear:

You need to

Brag that you can play better

Grab the cards

Make fun of their game

After the role play, discuss how it felt to have her criticize or barge in on their game.
Ask:

What was wrong with how she tried to join your game?

Did you like her grabbing your cards? Did her behavior make you want to play with her in the future?

7.4   Demonstrate the Right Way to Join a Group

NOTE: This role play should not be performed in front of the class. Doing so could embarrass the child and exacerbate his or her social anxiety.

For this role play, you again need a minimum three children. Instruct the newcomer to try to join the game, but instead of barging in, she is to try to join the game the right way. If you have three children, continue to pretend that the two are playing a card game or a board game. Instruct the newcomer to come up gradually on the game and to watch and wait for positive signs. The newcomer:

1. *Approaches* gradually to observe from the sidelines. (If it were a volleyball game, she would be near the middle of the court where she can comfortably watch both sides.)

2. She *greets* the others with a nod or a "Hi" while checking to see if anyone acknowledges her greeting.

3. She w*aits and watches* until she knows what the score is and how far along the game is or if it is almost over. (This waiting period can be between from one to five minutes or more.)

4. If it isn't clear who's winning or what the score is, the girl can *ask*, "Who's winning?" or "What's the score?"

5. Again, she *observes* the feedback. Did they readily tell her the score, or did they seem to not want to be bothered?

6. After watching a little longer, she *can give* someone a compliment after a good play, such as "Good play."

7. Again, she *observes* how the others respond to her.

8. If they aren't demonstrating friendly body language, she *does not ask* if she can play.

9. She *waits* until a member of the group gives her a **green** light (makes eye contact or asks her if she want to play when the game is over).

10. When the game is over, she *can offer* to join the team that lost the game or the one that has fewer players (often a strategy that boys use successfully).

After the role play is over and each child has an opportunity to be the newcomer, ask the children what they learned. Write down and go over their answers. Refer as necessary to the box "The Correct Way to Join an Ongoing Group."

The Correct Way to Join an Ongoing Group

Enter gradually and watch.

Small group: get within three feet.

Large activity, such as volleyball or basketball: sit on the sidelines near the middle of the court.

Greet the children, saying "Hi" or nodding.

Pay attention to see if you get a friendly response.

(No response is the same as an unfriendly response.)

Assess.

Wait and watch for a few minutes (two to five minutes).

Observe the game to see what the score is, who is playing well, and which side needs more help.

Make a comment or give a compliment, such as "Good shot" or "Way to go."

Wait and observe their reactions. *Wait* until a member of the group gives you a **green** light (makes eye contact or asks you if you want to play when the game is over).

When the game is over, you can offer to join the team that lost the game or the one that has fewer players (often a strategy that boys use successfully).

Summary for parent or teacher:
Coach the child on

1. Proximity
2. Eye contact
3. Waiting and making positive comments
4. Respecting nonverbal STOP signs

Successful children express interest in social contact. Children need to greet the group and engage in other-directed questions, comments, or compliments:

"What's the score?"
"That was a good throw!"
"That looks like fun."
"You're good at this."

Popular children show their interest but do not push themselves on other children. They look for an opening and either wait to be invited or ask gently if they can play if the children seem friendly. If not, they wait and watch or find another activity. Even popular children get refused 50 percent of the time. However, they don't take a refusal personally; they find someone else to play with or see if there is some activity they can do by themselves.

7.5   Inclusion or Exclusion?

Ask: *Do other children* have *to include you?*
Some children think that they have a right to be included. The truth is that children will exclude another child whom they view as too pushy or overbearing or if they think the child will ruin their game or their play. Despite school policies to the contrary, the children will find a way to exclude a child whom they don't like, even if they have to wait until the teacher on yard duty looks the other way.

Ask: *How do you handle it when other children say you can't join their game?*
This is a hard topic for children who take refusals personally (as a rejection). Because children often want to lash back at others for hurting them, you need to discuss the difference between refusal and rejection with the child. (This can be a topic for a classroom lesson as well.)

7.6   Rejection Versus Refusal

Ask: *Do you know the difference between refusal and rejection?*
Discuss the box "The Difference Between Refusal and Rejection."

The Difference Between Refusal and Rejection

A **refusal** is situational. It usually means that now isn't a good time. It usually isn't a comment about you and your personality or characteristics.

A **rejection** is based on personality traits, abilities or lack thereof, or behaviors. If a child doesn't play a sport well, others may not want him or her to join their team. Sometimes children are rejected because they break rules, are oppositional, or are annoying and don't stop when asked.

Adjusting the language appropriately, discuss these ideas with the child:

Children who have good self-esteem take a refusal at face value. It doesn't threaten their self-esteem. They don't translate "This isn't a good time for you to join our group" into "We don't like you."

You will be refused 50 percent of the time. Don't take it personally. Focus on the people who like you.

Children who have poor self-esteem assume that when the other children refuse them, it is because of some innate characteristic or personality defect. They take it as a rejection, and whether their perception is true or false, it tends to further lower their self-esteem.

There are situations when children do reject another child.

- Among children who play team sports, they often will not want to include any child who may threaten their ability to win. (This can be viewed as a refusal or a rejection depending on the child's self-esteem.)
- Children do reject a child who is very aggressive, doesn't follow the rules, insults others, is bossy, and in general ruins the game for the participants.

Sometimes adults insist that the children include a specific girl or boy. (That is, the adult overrides the objections of the children.) Unfortunately, this can backfire because of the resentment it can create. When a child is pushed into a group, the other children tend to avoid the child, and this can make the situation even worse for him or her.

Discuss the idea that all children are refused 50 percent of the time. Instead of getting their feelings hurt, they need to seek out other children and activities.

To conclude this discussion,
Ask:

Have you ever excluded anyone?
Why did you do it?

Why Kids May Refuse You

When a group of children refuse to let you join, it may be because

- It isn't a good time for them. The game just started.
- They may be involved in a game and do not want to start over.
- They may not want to include any new person.
- They may not think that you will add to their play (for example, they may think you don't have the skill or don't share their interests).
- They may think that you don't play the sport or game as well as their team does, and they may lose if they let you play with them.
- If they view you as annoying or disruptive, if you break rules and in general do not stop these behaviors when asked, the children may be refusing or rejecting you because they do not want to deal with your negative behaviors.

7.7 Groups and Cliques

By second and third grade, boys and girls start to play in same-gender groups exclusively and avoid interacting with members of the opposite sex. Boys often form groups based on their common interests in a sport, activity, or game. Their play is often based on rules. Girls' play is generally in smaller groups and is more focused on relationships (Maccoby, 1990; Maccoby & Jacklin, 1974). Girls' group behavior may have changed over the last twenty years, particularly with the significant increase in girls' participation in team sports. (In other words, their play may have become more rule based and concerned with winning.)

Boys and Their Play

Frequently, boys form groups around a sports team or common interest in a game. Because the goal of the group is to win, the team can be open to new members, particularly if the new boy excels in the activity or sport or has something new to share that the group values. In boys' groups, there is usually a hierarchy; often the leader, the "alpha male," is either the strongest, the best looking, or the most accomplished. Boys tend to have more rules in their play, and conflicts erupt when the rules are broken. Because their interest is in keeping the game going, boys often work out the conflicts (Maccoby, 1990).

As boys move into adolescence, their groups become more formalized. Boys often use teasing within the group (and without) to establish both their internal pecking order and external boundaries. With younger boys, the teasing is often name-calling. With older boys, it is more often disparaging comments about the victim's family (Frankel, 1996).

As hard as it is to manage, it is important for boys to learn to handle teasing. If a boy handles teasing well, his status is increased within the group, elevating him in the pecking order. A desirable response is to be able to laugh off teasing or joking. If the boy allows the teasing to get to him (for example, if he gets angry or cries), he loses status in the group and may be subjected to more teasing. (See Lesson Eight.)

Girls and Their Play

Younger girls play in smaller groups frequently focused on a toy, doll, or game. Their play is often imaginary and utilizes their relationship skills. Maccoby (1990) found that girls' play was based on cooperation and that conflicts frequently ended their play. Girls placed greater value on cooperation, listening, caretaking, and the relationship-maintaining activities of sharing, empathizing, and remembering events of significance to their friends.

The first longitudinal study of girls with ADHD (Faraone et al., 2000),[1] which measured the effects of ADHD on their development, concluded that girls with ADHD did **far worse than their peers and significantly worse than boys with ADHD,** who were more often diagnosed and treated as children. The girls had significant emotional problems and family issues; they most often had not been diagnosed as children. I have speculated (Giler, 2000) that one reason that girls with ADHD fair so poorly may be that they often fail to master the rapport-building skills that come more naturally to those who aren't impulsive or inattentive or who don't have issues with aggression. Some girls with ADHD find it easier to be friends with boys, who are more tolerant of direct confrontations and expect less "rapport talk" than girls do (Maccoby, 1990; Giler, 2000; Simmons, 2002).

How ADHD May Affect Girls and Their Friendships

Girls with ADHD may have friendship problems because of their

Distractibility, which can lead to being late, forgetting appointments, or failing to keep secrets

Impulsivity and hyperactivity, which can lead to being bossy, aggressive, or outspoken; putting others down; or ignoring others' wants

Poor mood regulation and modulation of expression, which can lead to expressing too much anger or negative emotion

---

As girls move into adolescence (and for some this transition occurs in the fifth grade), they start bonding with others in small social groups that become friendship circles (as opposed to the more formal, organized cliques in junior high and high school). By fifth grade, these friendship circles morph into small groups that share a common interest—for example, being on the same sports team, taking the same dance class, or having similar tastes or interest in fashion.

Shared values or being of the same religion or ethnic background can also forge bonds. Girls who are friends often adopt a similar style of dress or hairstyle, or use similar phrases or tone of voice. The girls are connected through a network of friendships. They often bond by sharing secrets with each other (Frankel, 1996; Wiseman, 2002).

Sometimes, joining a group requires that the new girl know someone who is already in the group. Frequently the new girl has something that is prized by the group, whether it is a talent or a connection through some activity with one of the girls.

Girls tend to socialize in smaller groups of two or three, and often get together after school. The current way of staying connected is to meet up in cyberspace, where they network with each other on such sites as MySpace or Facebook. Whether they are talking, texting, or instant messaging, many girls use technology to set up future dates and activities. They also share gossip and can use networking sites to both include and exclude others.

As girls become adolescents, their associational groups look more like cliques, which often adopt similar styles of dress and speech patterns (with shared phrases, intonation, or cadence). Some groups have a recognized leader. Sometimes it's the leader's (the Queen Bee's) job to control new membership. Inclusion and exclusion define the boundaries of the group. Sometimes a member, a "wannabe," will tease or reject another girl to show her loyalty to the group (Wiseman, 2002). If the group is well formed or has a strong leader, a new girl will have trouble joining without support from the Queen Bee.

7.8   When Your Child Cannot Join a Group (for Parents)

When your child cannot join a group, your role is to help him or her come up with alternative social activities. Adults cannot insist that a group include their children and should help redirect their children into other activities (or groups) in which membership is based on their participation (for example, a theater production or the school's band). Some children with SN are not really comfortable with groups (of any kind) and find their hidden rules and communication styles too confusing; if your child prefers to be alone, you will have to seek out solitary activities to interest him or activities that require less interaction. (To help your child with the skills for joining a group, see Section 7.4.) Refer to Exercise 8: Finding Neighborhood Activities: A Parent's Job.

After-school activities offer your child other places to socialize that may be easier and less challenging. A benefit of after-school activities is that if children make any mistakes, they don't damage their reputation at school. Participating in sports, scouts, theater productions, martial arts, orchestra or band, church groups, after-school employment (for example, babysitting), or volunteering at nonprofit organizations all offer social alternatives to children. Remember, having some friends outside of school can compensate for not having friends in school, even if some of the friends are older or younger children or adults.

Exercise 30: Practice Joining an Ongoing Group

Step One: Enter on the sidelines and watch.

Step Two: Say something friendly.

Step Three: Assess the children by reading their body language.

    Are they friendly?

    Do they look at you and smile?

    Do they acknowledge you, or are they ignoring you?

Step Four: Give compliments or ask questions.

Step Five: Wait for a **yes** signal; for example, they ask you to join them or respond to you in a friendly way.

Step Six: Wait for a natural break. If they children aren't friendly, find another activity.

Remember: Other children do not *have* to include you.

★ Respect other people and their desires to be alone or with someone else. ★

Exercise 31: Defining the Groups at School

Spend a little time observing the different groups that gather together during recess and see if you can identify the different groups or cliques at your school. Here are some of the groups that might be at your school. Do you see yourself fitting in with any of these groups?

- Popular children
- Athletes, jocks
- Smart kids, geeks
- Computer kids, nerds
- Musicians, members of band, orchestra, or choir
- Artsy types (kids who are involved in theater or art)
- Countercultural kids: punks, rockers, hippies, or freaks
- Ethnic or religiously defined group
- Groups based on gender identity
- Special interest clubs, chess, photography
- Emos—emotional kids
- Loners
- Regular kids

Note for Lesson Seven

1. The first big study of girls with ADHD (Faraone et al., 2000) indicated that girls with ADHD have poorer family relationships, are more frequently addicted to substances than their male counterparts, and often have significant learning problems, although few received remedial services in their schools. The study indicated that 50 percent of the girls in the sample had significant secondary psychological problems (co-occurring conditions) and significant learning problems. In Giler (2000), I suggested that girls with ADHD might be worse at communicating with other females than their peers (and hence may be more isolated), because female communication involves more cooperation and rapport talk than girls with impulse problems may be willing or able to do. Girls with ADHD often find themselves out on the social periphery as neglected or rejected children. (See notes 1 and 2 in Chapter One; Cowen, Pederson, Babigan, Izzo, & Trost, 1973, on rejected children; and Laugeson & Frankel, 2010, on changing a bad reputation.)

Dealing with Teasing

Teasing is prevalent and hard for most children to handle. Children with SN often fail to see that there are different types of teasing: sometimes teasing is part of a friendly interchange; at other times, it is unfriendly and mean. Figuring out the type of teasing requires that children be able to accurately surmise the nature of the teasing in the context of the current relationship between the parties (which often requires using social memory). Children also have to correctly infer the other person's intent, which involves mind-reading correctly the meta-message conveyed both in the body language and tone. This chapter offers some tips for how to sort out the three forms of teasing and recommends how children should respond to each type.

8.1 Why Children Tease Others

Introduce the topic by asking:
> *Why do you think children tease each other?*

Refer to the box "Why Children Tease Others."

Discuss teasing by asking the child what they already know about it.

Ask: *Do children who tease others feel good about themselves?*
> Answer: Not usually

Ask: *Who gets teased?*
> Answer: Children who are little different

Ask: *Why does teasing bother us?*
> Answer: It hurts our feelings because we feel insecure about ourselves.

Ask if the child has experienced friendly teasing:

What happens if a friend teases you about something that you like (or have accepted) about yourself?

Answer: Most of the time, I don't get upset. I just think he is joking and sometimes I laugh with him.

Why Children Tease Others

- To feel better about themselves
- To deal with jealous feelings
- To feel superior
- To make you feel bad
- To gain status (in groups)
- To appear funny or clever
- To handle jealousy
- To deal with their anger
- To tell you to stop doing something annoying
- To correct rude or embarrassing behavior (for example, body odor, space violations, hogging the airtime)

Friendly teasing is a form of joking and, as such, is commonly used among friends to communicate with each other. Although teasing can be friendly, there is also a form that isn't friendly at all (put-down humor). If a child does not know how to handle the teasing and reacts with a lot of emotion, he will often get teased more by the other children. A child benefits from having a strategy that enables him to handle teasing (by showing the others it doesn't bother him). This is one of the few ways in which a child can circumvent being the target of more teasing. Teasing remains a hot topic among parents and school personnel. (See Lesson Ten on cyber-bullying as well.)

8.2   Three Major Types of Teasing

Discuss the three different types of teasing (refer to the box "Three Major Types of Teasing and How to Respond to Each").

Three Major Types of Teasing and How to Respond to Each

1. **"Knock it off" teasing:** uses sarcasm or exaggeration to get the child to stop; it addresses two categories, rude or embarrassing behavior and bothersome behaviors.

Rude or embarrassing behavior:

- Body odor
- Burping
- Farting
- Making weird noises or gestures
- Telling babyish jokes (bathroom humor)

Bothersome behavior:

- Talking too much (perseverating)
- Interrupting
- Bumping into someone
- Sharing something that was embarrassing or private

Correct response: The child is supposed to change his or her behavior (stop doing the identified behavior).

2. **Friendly teasing:** uses sarcasm or exaggeration to point out flaws in appearance, bodily functions, or behavior. It often focuses on awkward moments when the child, often unintentionally, commits a social gaff, a social error. To the child (if this is uncharacteristic behavior) it may be embarrassing, and he or she may not appreciate being reminded of it.

Friendly teasing

- Occurs between friends or family members
- Targets behavior that others assume you can accept about yourself

Comedians use this kind of humor, called spoof or slapstick humor, but instead of targeting an individual, they often make fun of groups of people.

Correct response: The child is supposed to laugh at the jibe (and show that she has a sense of humor about her mistakes).

3. **Status teasing** (put-down humor):

- Often occurs in front of other children who are in a group.[1]
- Can be about character flaws, religious beliefs, nonnormative behaviors, or the social or economic status of the child or his or her family members.
- Makes the assumption that putting down the child will make the teaser look better to the group.[2]
- Can be used as a "hazing" ritual, in which the teased child's response can determine if the group accepts him or her. The child's response can lower his or her status within group or can be a criterion for total exclusion.

Correct response: The child should ignore or make a joke of status and put-down teasing.

NOTE: The following is a good group exercise for classroom teachers. Ask the children for examples of any of these types of teasing that they have seen used or have personally experienced.

1. "Knock it off" teasing
2. Friendly teasing
3. Status teasing using put-down humor

8.3   Why Children Use Status Teasing (or Put-Down Humor)

Usually children who tease others are insecure about themselves. They are trying to gain something by putting the other child down, whether it is approval of a group or attention from someone else. Although some girls do this type of teasing, it is much more common among boys, often beginning during third and fourth grade and continuing into adulthood. Sometimes status teasing is used as a form of hazing, and how well the targeted boy handles the teasing either increases or decreases his status in the group (see note 2 for this lesson).

8.4   Boys and Status Teasing

The way status teasing works is that a "wannabe" boy targets a second boy whom he identifies as weaker than he is. (For example, the second boy has a trait or mannerism that is different, such as being slower or less athletic.) The first boy teases the second boy, usually in front of his group. If the second boy swallows the bait and reacts negatively to the teasing, the first boy's status is increased in the group. This type of teasing can be viewed as a challenge; the second boy is supposed to show that he is "cool," "strong," and able to "handle it." If the second boy fails to handle the teasing well, his status is diminished in the group, and he will likely be on the receiving end of more teasing.

We see this same phenomenon in primate societies in which the alpha male often uses his display of dominance to establish that he is the strongest leader. Gorillas and other primates don't usually fight to see who is the most dominant; instead they puff themselves up, roar, beat their chests, and show off their strength. This bluffing behavior usually works; the strongest male dominates, and the weaker males retreat and acknowledge the alpha male as the leader. The whole bluffing phenomenon is referred to as a *dominance display*.

It appears that adolescent males (and adults) use status teasing and how well the boy handles it as a form of dominance display to determine social resilience or strength. If the boy is witty or shows that the teasing doesn't bother him, it elevates his status within the group.

8.5　Evaluating the Type of Teasing

Teachers, parents, and counselors need to help children come up with strategies to handle teasing. The first step is to help the child identify which type of teasing is being directed at him or her. Knowing the type of teasing enables the child to come up with different strategies. This is a good role-play activity for parents and counselors. Important note: this is *not* a good classroom activity for teachers.

Help the child evaluate the type of teasing by asking him or her these questions:

What kind of teasing is this?

What kind of relationship do you have with the child who is teasing you?

Do you think the child is asking you to stop doing _____ (fill in behavior)?

Discuss the box "Figuring Out the Type of Teasing." It can be read to the child.

Figuring Out the Type of Teasing

The type of teasing often depends on the relationship (past and present) that you have with the child who is teasing you.

1. "Knock it off" teasing

Ask yourself these questions:

Have I done something that the other child is finding annoying and is asking me to STOP?

Has the child teased me in the past about "stopping," and have I ignored his or her request to stop?

If the answer is yes to either question, you need to stop doing the offending behavior.

(continued)

(continued)

2. Friendly teasing
Ask yourself these questions:

Have we been friends in the past?

Do I think this child likes me?

Is his or her body language friendly?

If I knew that this child liked me, would I think that this teasing is funny?

Is the teasing about something that I can accept about myself (for example, a funny hairdo or an odd favorite outfit)?

Can I laugh about this targeted behavior, mannerism, or fact about myself?

Is the child who is teasing me similar to me? (Do we have similar values, attributes, or mannerisms?) Are we part of the same racial, ethnic, or religious group?

If you answer yes to any of these questions, the teasing may be friendly.

3. Status teasing using put-down humor
Ask yourself these questions:

Am I being teased in front of a group?

Have I ever been friends with this person or others in his or her group?

Do I sometimes hang out with this group of children?

If the answer is yes to any of these questions, how you handle the teasing is part of a "hazing ritual" and can influence where you end up in the group's pecking order.

If you have no prior relationship with the teaser, assume that his or her intention is to be mean and hurtful. Although this is the type of teasing that often elicits violent responses, this is a no-win situation. If you fight, you get kicked out of school, and you aren't going to change the person's mind whatever you do, as this form of teasing comes from bigotry or prejudice.

8.6   The Wrong Way to Handle Teasing

One of the best ways to help children come up with strategies to handle teasing is for them to role-play how they might respond to the different forms of teasing. In this section, the adult demonstrates what won't work well. This exercise can be done in a classroom, but I recommend that it be done by a parent or counselor in a smaller, more private setting.

Ask the child to tease you about your shirt or blouse. Demonstrate handling teasing the wrong way by

- Getting angry
- Calling her a name
- Teasing her back
- Hitting her (pretending to act it out)

Ask: *Why don't these responses work very well?*
Answers can include the following:

- It makes the other child angry.
- The other child will want to hurt you back.
- The child might tell other children how you responded.

Discuss the concept of responding aggressively when you have been attacked, and what usually happens. (Does it escalate into a bigger fight?)[3]
Ask: *What is the goal of teasing?*
Answer: To get you upset

Wrong Ways to Handle Teasing

- Name-calling
- Telling the teacher (for older children)
- Hitting
- Crying
- Withdrawing
- Getting angry

8.7 Three Strategies to Handle Teasing

Say:
> *The only way to win with teasing is to show the children who are teasing you that what they say doesn't matter to you.*

There are three ways you can respond to teasing:

1. Ignore the words.

Demonstrate how to ignore someone:

- Say nothing in response.
- Don't look at the child.
- Keep doing what you are doing.
- Ask a redirecting question about a totally different topic, pretending that you had not heard the jibe.

2. Agree with the words.

Demonstrate how to agree with the words:

Teaser: "Boy, does your hair look silly."
You: "Yes, it didn't do what I wanted it to do today."

3. Agree by making a joke out of the teasing.

"You mean my new fifties look [laughing]?"
"Don't you think it looks great?"

Ask:
What message do children get if you

Ignore them?
Agree with them?
Make a joke out of their teasing?

Answer: They see that the teasing doesn't matter to you and that you aren't going to get upset.[4]
Ask:
If you react, will you get teased more?
Answer: Yes

8.8   Role-Play Being Teased

The most effective way to learn how to handle teasing is to role-play how you should respond to teasing. This needs to be done in a safe setting because to be effective, the child needs to be teased about something that would really hurt him or make him feel bad.

NOTE: *Because of the sensitive nature of this exercise, it is* not *a good classroom exercise. It should be done in a safe setting, such as in a small group or with a parent.*

The adult should start off by volunteering to be teased first. The first step is to establish "safe" boundaries: you clearly define to the child the topics that are "off-limits."

Begin by asking the child to say one teasing comment to you. You model handling the comment by using one of these three methods:

1. Ignoring the comment
2. Agreeing with the comment
3. Making a joke of the comment

Ask the child to go next. Make sure that he or she understands that the idea is to not react to teasing. Have the child define the off-limits topics.

The teasing should target a fairly safe behavior or an aspect of the child's appearance. It is helpful to use something that he thinks he can change if he wished, such as a hairstyle or an outfit he is wearing. Remember that the goal here is to have the child experience success while handling teasing.

Congratulate the child on his or her use of one of these techniques.

If the child becomes upset, remind her of her good qualities and that this is just a role play.

★ For parents: This is a good time to remind your child that we all have good qualities and all have weaknesses; it takes a strong person to admit one's own weaknesses. This is also an appropriate time to share any experiences you had being teased while growing up and how you handled them.

Three Ways to Handle Teasing

1. Ignore the words by asking a redirecting question.
2. Agree with the comment.
3. Agree with the comment and make a joke out of it.

8.9   When Jokes Aren't Funny: The Rules of Humor

Discuss these ideas:

Joking is a common way for people to communicate with each other. Although most children can pick up on the "hidden rule" of how to tell a joke and to whom, these rules often elude the child with SN.

Demonstrate the wrong way to tell a joke:

- Announce that you are going to tell a joke.
- Laugh to yourself about the joke.

- Announce the punch line.
- Explain the joke.

Ask the child to evaluate what you did wrong.
Discuss the box "Rules for Telling Jokes."

Rules for Telling Jokes

Do not introduce the joke by saying, "I've got a joke."

Do not explain the joke.

Do not introduce the punch line.

Do not explain why the joke is funny.

Do not be the first one to laugh at the joke.

Obey the Rule of Equals (discussed in Section 8.10).

Because it is important to know how to respond to someone else's jokes, discuss the strategy of laughing even if the child doesn't get the joke.
Discuss these points:

If you do not get a joke, asking others to explain it

- *Can be annoying*
- *Draws attention to your weaknesses (that you didn't get it) or might make others think you are slow or different in some way*

A better strategy is to laugh anyway, and later ask a friend or parent to explain why the joke was funny.

Although being good at telling jokes can increase a child's status in a group, the converse is also true: telling babyish jokes (for example, using bathroom humor) can lower his or her status because others might think the child is immature, crude, or insensitive. It is important to obey the Rule of Equals.

8.10   The Rule of Equals

Sigmund Freud said years ago that when jokes are funny, it is because they address something that is partially true. Although joking can be a way to get you to correct your behavior, most often it is a way to entertain and amuse others, who, you hope, share your sense of humor and values. However, if you tell a joke that makes fun of a character flaw or a trait associated with an ethnic or religious group, it may not be funny; it may in fact be very offensive. The person may take this kind of joke as a put-down. The unspoken rule is that you can only tell a joke to someone who is similar to you.

Ask: *When is it OK to tell a joke about a character flaw?*

If the child has trouble answering, ask: *Have you ever had someone make fun of you, but you thought it was OK?*

Discuss the idea that jokes about characteristics are not funny unless you know that (1) the person accepts this characteristic in himself or herself and (2) the person doesn't mind being the butt of the joke. In other words, you can only make fun of a person's flaws if the other person knows that you like him or her. If the person is at all sensitive about the character flaw or characteristic, he or she won't think the joke is funny.

Discuss the Rule of Equals: *Like can tease like.*

If you are not of the same

- Race
- Gender
- Ethnicity
- Religion
- Disability

do not make fun of any trait related to race, gender, ethnicity, religion, or disability.

In other words, people who are in the same group or who share the same disability or personal characteristics can make fun of their flaws or character traits, whereas others who are outside the group *cannot.* If you do not share the same characteristic, flaw, or belief system, you risk being seen as crude, ill-mannered, or downright insulting.

(Admittedly, skilled comedians break this rule, but they are very good at judging their audiences and covering up quickly if they make a mistake.)

The Rules for Telling Jokes

Rule 1: The Rule of Equals: Never make fun of a trait, race, ethnic group, religion, or disability if you don't have the same trait or are not a member of the same group (gender, race, religion, ethnic group, disability).

Discuss with children how to evaluate their audience.

Some important questions to ask are:

Why are you together? Is this a party or a general gathering at school? If you are at school, the jokes should be cleaner and broader in their appeal.

(continued)

(continued)

Are you with others who are of the same similar race, religion, age, or physical limitation? Use the Rule of Equals.

Do you have the same status (for example, are both girls, are equally matched in academics or sports)? Use the Rule of Equals.

Are you the same age? Use the Rule of Equals.

Rule 2: Never make fun of people who have more status than you do.

A teacher may be able to tease another teacher or a child, but a child *cannot and should not* tease a teacher or the principal. This may true in some families as well, in which the parents can tease the child, but the child cannot tease the parent.

Rule 3: If in doubt, don't.

If you have any doubt about who your audience is or the appropriateness of a joke, don't tell it. This includes the appropriateness of bathroom humor or telling sexual jokes or jokes about gender identity. These jokes can offend others.[5]

Exercise 32: Figuring Out the Type of Teasing

If you get teased, ask yourself the following questions to see if you can figure out the intention behind the teasing.

1. Is the child telling me to *stop doing something,* such as

   Talking—perseverating (talking on and on), telling silly or inappropriate jokes

   Burping

   Farting

   Making weird noises or gestures

   Having offensive body odor

2. Is it friendly teasing?

   Have we been friendly in the past?

   Can I laugh about the comment or trait?

3. Is this status teasing or put-down humor?

   Is the person teasing me in front of his or her group?

   Does putting me down make the person look better to his or her peers?

   Is the person teasing me about character flaws, religious beliefs, or social status?

Respond to all teasing by doing one of three things:

1. Ignoring it (change topic, bringing up something else or asking a question to redirect the teaser to something else)
2. Making a joke of it ("Yeah, it's Halloween, you know.")
3. Agreeing with it ("Yeah, it is a weird hairdo. I thought it would look better than it does.")

★ Under no circumstances attack the attacker back. ★

Notes for Lesson Eight

1. Whereas status teasing happens only in front of a group of other children, a child can be teased with the intent of putting down the child, her family, or her religious or social group. It is solely meant to be destructive and targets real flaws, including derogatory comments about personal beliefs, social status, or even disabilities. These comments are from a child who is not from the same ethnic, religious, or social group, or clan.

2. Put-down teasing is what Berne (1964) called a variant of "I'm OK but you're not," because the assumption is that only one of us can be OK. This concept is also fundamental to the economic theory called the *zero-sum game*, the premise of which is that if someone wins, the other one has to lose.

3. The concept of symmetrical transactions is that if one responds in kind to an aggressive act, the exchange will increase the aggressiveness and the intensity of the discord. It is referred to as *escalation* and is the most common way that conflicts increase in their intensity and scope (Watzlawick, Breavin, & Jackson, 1967).

4. These methods are demonstrated in the training DVD *From Acting Out to Fitting In* (Giler, 1998b), both by Dr. Giler and by children who participated in ADDept groups.

5. Because telling inappropriate jokes often gets children into trouble, this topic is appropriate to discuss here. Boys often tell jokes labeled as bathroom humor, and although these jokes may be funny when the children are in third grade, they may be seen as too immature to a child of twelve.

Managing Anger

When children with SN get hurt, they often engage in black-and-white thinking and attribute the worst possible intentions to the other child. What started off as a joke can escalate into a hurt feeling that morphs into a fight or a conflict that never gets resolved. In this lesson, some cognitive strategies are introduced to help children recognize their anger triggers and to define some alternative ways to respond. However, some children with SN can't control their outbursts, so adults need a containment strategy to handle those outbursts. The last strategy, apologizing, is a conflict resolution skill that children with SN need; they need to how to apologize when they have offended someone by their words, actions, or deeds, whether they were intentional or not.

9.1   Why Do We Get Angry?

Note: This can be a classroom discussion.
Say:
> *Anger is a difficult emotion to control because when we are angry, we are usually hurt as well.*

Ask: *What are some of the things that can make you angry?*
The answers should include

When someone hits or pushes me

When I've been teased

When I've been excluded

When I don't get what I want

When someone takes something that is mine

When something is not fair

When I can't go out with my friends

When I don't get to go play

When someone shares a secret of mine

When someone embarrasses me in front of others

Although we can't control the things that make us angry, we can *control how we react. Controlling how we react is important because what we say and do has consequences.*

9.2 Why Should Children Control Their Anger?

Ask:

Why is it important to control what you do when you are angry ?
Answers can include:

You might hurt someone verbally or physically.

You might say something that you can't take back later (and may regret).

Ask:

Can you give me an example of something you did when you were angry that you regretted later?
Possible answers:

I hurt someone.

I called someone a name.

I took something that belonged to someone else.

I broke something.

I hurt myself.

Ask:

Why do you think you might regret some angry actions?
Possible answers:

You lose friends.

People withdraw from you.

You break something you cared about.

You can hurt someone and he or she won't forgive you.

You hurt yourself.

You get a bad reputation.

9.3   The Hot-Tempered Child

Some children with SN, particularly those who don't have a lot of control over their impulses, often do or say things that can be very hurtful to others. Sometimes they regret their actions. But some children stay angry so long that they end up feeling that their actions are justified. Although all anger management programs use cognitive methods to help children (and adults) recognize their anger "triggers" and to recognize and rate their physiological responses (usually in the early stage when an explosion can be averted), the

> **What we say and do with our anger can permanently affect us and others.**

assumption is that children (and adults) will be able to describe and choose alternative behaviors. However, it is important to recognize that there are those for whom these strategies will not work.

There are children (and adults) who have "hot tempers" and who easily "see red." When they are younger, they will need to be contained when they are angry and removed from the source of their anger so that they will not hurt the other child or themselves. This method is more a form of damage control than an anger management technique. Some impulsive children will benefit from taking medication that can slow down their reactions or even alter their negative perceptions of the events or persons that caused them to be angry in the first place.

9.4   Identifying Physical Responses to Anger

People have an automatic response to anger, and for many impulsive children with SN, this response can arise very quickly Their heartbeat increases, and blood flows to the brain stem and to the large muscle groups in the legs and arms. An angry person is more mentally alert, and his or her body is ready to fight or to flee. Unfortunately, many children with Asperger's Syndrome and ADHD may actually like this side effect of being angry because it truly wakes up their brains.

Discuss the physiology of anger and the autonomic nervous system.

The body's nervous system controls our reaction to anger, and for some of us, this process happens very quickly. For many of us, the cooling-off period may take twenty to twenty-five minutes or even a few hours.

9.5   Identifying the Child's Anger Style

Ask:

What happens to you when you get angry? Do you get over it quickly, do you stay calm and reason it out, or does it take a lot to get you angry and then you stay angry for a long time?

Discuss the different ways people handle their anger (see the box "Different Ways People Handle Anger").

> ## Different Ways People Handle Anger
>
> **Explosive type:** explodes before he or she thinks about it
>
> **Aggressive type:** attacks quickly like a shark and blames the other person
>
> **Problem solver:** tries to see the other person's point of view and tries to compromise
>
> **Avoider:** hates conflict and will do whatever the other person wants

Ask:
Which style do you use to express your anger?
Do you know how long your cooling-off period is?

9.6 Identifying Anger Triggers

Children who are impulsive often have hot tempers. It is important that they learn to catch themselves during the first stage of their anger response.
Discuss what makes the child angry. Use Exercise 33: What Makes You Angry? Discuss all the possible triggers and have the child write his or her own list. It is useful to rate the importance of an issue, with 0 being not very important and 7 being very important. If you are dealing with younger children, you can use colors to represent their reactions as well. Some teachers like to use the Incredible 5 Point Scale (Buron & Curtis, 2003), which uses a thermometer model to identify angry feelings and rate their intensity.

9.7 Checking Out the Other Person's Intentions

The easiest way to manage an anger response is to change one's thinking. Many children with SN perceive that the action or words that offended them happened because the offending child intended to hurt them. This is often not true. Children often forget that they have had a number of positive interactions with the offending child. Instead of seeing a bump as an accident, it is often seen as an intentional push. If children assume that the other child intended to hurt them, their anger is justified. But what if they are wrong? Sometimes children project negative intentions when they are not there.

Much of this advice to the child is academic and may go flying out the window when the child is really angry. When a situation arises, see if you can problem-solve with the child. The most important part is to encourage the child to see the situation differently by asking:

What if the person didn't intend to hurt you but was thoughtless or careless; would you still be as angry?

What if the incident was an accident?

Using "what if" questions can help the child think through the situation to see if there is another explanation that may make the "wrongdoing" less hurtful. Because seeing another child's perspective is difficult for many children with SN, this is an important practice.

9.8   Handling Anger the Wrong Way

Note: This can be an individual or group exercise. (Wording here reflects group work.)
Ask the children to imagine the following situation and to think about how they might handle it.
You are playing with a toy and some children come and take it from you. What do you do?
Ask the children to identify some of the wrong ways of handling the situation.
Answers can include the following:

I could call them a name.

I could hit them.

I could grab the toy back.

Discuss what might happen if the children acted out their anger the wrong way.
Possible answers:

The other child might hit me back.

The other child might call me a name back.

The other child might tell other people that I was mean.

Ask:
What would be a better solution?

Possible answers:

I could ask for the toy back.

I could let them play with the toy and choose another toy.

I could make a deal that we can share the toy and play a game together.

Discuss the ideas in the box "Anger Principles."

Anger Principles

- Sometimes you can't control getting angry.
- If you cannot control yourself, it is often better to take a break or get some time away to cool down.
- If you say something when you are angry that is mean or hurtful, you may not be able to take it back. (Sometimes it has permanent consequences.)
- Anger scares people, and sometimes they react by getting angry back at you or by withdrawing from you.

9.9   Seven Steps to Process Anger

Discuss these steps to use when angry, referring to the box "Seven Steps for Handling Anger."

Seven Steps for Handling Anger

1. **Identify feelings.** Think about what you are feeling. Are you jealous? Scared? Hurt?
2. **Reflect.** Did the person intend to hurt you? ("Maybe not.")
3. **Consider.** Did the person intend to hurt you? Ask yourself, "Did I hurt him or her first?" You might be unaware of something you said or did to hurt the other person. Or is it possible that the person is mad at you because he or she asked you to stop doing something and you didn't?
4. **Question.** "How important is this to me? Is it something that I can overlook?"

5. **Think.** Ask yourself, "What are my choices? Do I fight back? Retreat? Apologize?" If I'm really worked up, maybe I should take a break and think about it.
6. **Take a break.** If you get worked up easily, you need to take a step back from the situation by leaving the room or the house. If it takes you thirty minutes to cool down, take a thirty-minute walk or go for a run.
7. **Discuss.** After you have cooled down, talk to the other child about what made you angry; use "I" statements instead of attacking the other child or making him or her wrong.

Discuss and practice using "I" statements.

One of the best ways to discuss events that led to a fight is to share what you thought occurred or what you felt that made you angry.

When you use an "I" statement, you share your feelings or thoughts with a sentence starting with "I ..." instead of using an attacking, blaming statement such as "you did ..."or "you were ..." "I" statements refer to specific actions rather than characteristics of the other person.

Do say: "I got really angry at you when you took my toy. I didn't like it nor did I think it was fair."

Do not say: "You were really mean and selfish."

Do say: "I didn't like it when you took the toy. I thought it was my turn."

Do not say: "You cheater!" or "You always take my things!"

The other child will always listen better if you don't bring him or her in to the statement by saying "You are" or "You did." Even if you don't intend to blame the other person, he or she will hear blame anyway and most likely defend himself or herself.

9.10   Role-Play Handling Anger

Discuss the same situation described in Section 9.8, except now you can talk about and demonstrate handling the anger in a positive way.

Ask the children to imagine that they are playing with a toy and someone comes and takes it from them. What do they do?

Review the box in Section 9.9, "Seven Steps for Handling Anger." Also discuss the list in the following box, "Safe Ways to Deal with Anger," which acknowledges that sometimes the cognitive approach doesn't work.

Safe Ways to Deal with Anger

When the child is so angry that he can't control his reaction, these are some safer ways to get the child to calm down. This advice is for parents and teachers to redirect the child by

- **Venting.** Have the child hit a pillow, go for a run, throw a basketball, hit a punching bag, or yell at an imaginary person.
- **Sidestepping a power struggle.** If you see that a child is already agitated, do not bring up a something that will make it worse. Change the subject.
- **Taking a break and doing something physical.** Have the child go for a walk or a run, or ask him to do an errand for you.
- **Discovering the hurt behind the anger.** Encourage the child to examine her feelings; her anger may shift to sadness or hurt.
- **Turning the anger into action.** See if you can help the child figure out if he can do something constructive with his energy.
- **Reframing the message received.** This requires that the child step outside of her frame of reference by identifying the trigger or trying to see the situation from the other person's point of view. As an example, if your dad comes home in a bad mood and yells at you, instead of taking it personally, check to see if he had a bad day at work or if something else is bothering him.

9.11   When There Is an Outburst

There is subgroup among children with ADHD and Asperger's Syndrome who find it very hard to control their anger. Some, as mentioned earlier, find anger exciting, as it stimulates their brains and makes them very alert. Some children have very reactive nervous systems. They react so quickly that there isn't much time for them to go through any of the steps for handling anger.

Adults need to have a strategy for damage control, to protect the child from hurting himself or herself, hurting someone else, or damaging or destroying property. If you see that the child is starting to lose control (the child has passed the rumination stage and is now starting to actively vent his or her anger), it is important to try to remove the child from the situation. Sometimes distraction works (for example, giving the child a different task), but more often, the child needs a safe place to vent his or her anger so no one gets hurt.

An excellent resource is *Asperger's Syndrome and Difficult Moments* (Myles & Southwick, 2005). Myles suggests that an anger outburst can only be averted if caught during the "rumbling" phase. This is the first stage of anger when children start to fidget, swear, curse, and ruminate on the affront done to them. If children can be distracted at this point, an outburst can be stopped. However, if they cannot be distracted or talked down, 75 to 80 percent of them will go on to have a meltdown or outburst. Myles's method for containment is exceptionally good, and can help both teachers and parents with a child who is prone to having meltdowns.

9.12   Apologizing

Discuss:

Apologizing is an important skill. We all make mistakes and hurt others whether we intend to or not. We need to know how to say, "I'm sorry." Sometimes when we get angry, we say things we don't really mean, and the best thing to do if we have done that is to apologize to the person as soon as possible.

Discuss the box "Seven Steps to an Apology." Ask the child if she can think of a time that she did something that she thought was wrong. How did she apologize? Did she do all of these steps? (See Exercise 35: Practice Apologizing.)

Seven Steps to an Apology

1. **Admit the mistake.** "I know I was wrong when I . . ."
2. **Explain why it occurred.** "I was not being considerate . . ."
3. **Acknowledge hurting feelings.** "I realize I hurt your feelings."
4. **Apologize.** "I'm sorry I hurt your feelings."
5. **Affirm the relationship.** "I still want to be your friend."
6. **Try to correct the mistake.** "What can I do to make it up to you?"
7. **Adjust.** Change your behavior so that you don't make the same mistake again.

Exercise 33: What Makes You Angry?

For each of the following situations, circle your anger level, with 1 being only slightly angry and 6 being extremely angry.

Someone tells on you.

    1   2   3   4   5   6

You want a toy and don't get it.

    1   2   3   4   5   6

A friend doesn't invite you to a party.

    1   2   3   4   5   6

A friend breaks your toy.

    1   2   3   4   5   6

No one wants to play with you.

    1   2   3   4   5   6

You are accused of something you didn't do.

    1   2   3   4   5   6

You lose money.

    1   2   3   4   5   6

You do something well and no one notices.

    1   2   3   4   5   6

Someone teases you.

      1   2   3   4   5   6

You're told you can't join a game.

      1   2   3   4   5   6

Someone gets you in trouble.

      1   2   3   4   5   6

Your mother makes you do chores.

      1   2   3   4   5   6

You don't get to do what you want.

      1   2   3   4   5   6

You don't do well at school or in a sport.

      1   2   3   4   5   6

Exercise 34: Handling Anger Differently

Think of something that made you angry in the last week or two. How did you handle the situation?

Think about the ways that you would have liked to handle the situation and write down what you would like to have said or done differently.

1. **Identify feelings.** What was I feeling? Was I jealous? Scared? Hurt?
2. **Reflect and consider.** Did the person intend to hurt me? Did I hurt him or her first? Was the person mad at me because he or she asked me to stop doing something and I didn't?
3. **Ask yourself what you would do differently.** If I could go back and start over, I would change what I did by _____ (for example, waiting, going for a walk, doing exercise, taking a break, using "I" statements).
   "If I had used 'I' statements, I would have said...

I _____

_____

_____

_____

_____ "

I _____

_____

_____

_____

_____ "

Exercise 35: Practice Apologizing

Think of something that you said or did that hurt someone else. Think of how you tried to make up with this friend. Circle all the steps you did when you apologized. Write out what you could have done differently. (Remember, it is never too late to apologize.)

If you hurt someone and haven't apologized, think of what you would say to the child now. Try using these seven steps:

1. **Admit the mistake.** "I know I was wrong when I . . ."
2. **Explain why it occurred.** "I was not being considerate . . ."
3. **Acknowledge hurting feelings.** "I realize I hurt your feelings."
4. **Apologize.** "I'm sorry I hurt your feelings."
5. **Affirm the relationship.** "I still want to be your friend."
6. **Try to correct the mistake.** "What can I do to make it up to you?"

   _____

7. **Adjust.** I could change my behavior so that I don't make the same mistake again by doing _____

Children in Cyberspace: Old Rules, New Rules

In the last ten years, children's use of cyberspace has changed the landscape in which they interact with one another. It has increased children's ability to stay in touch with each other. Friends can be part of group chats, but children can also bar others from being part of their group talk. Children can also post unflattering information or pictures of another child on the Web without that child's knowledge or permission. For example, the dynamics between girls may not have changed: they still may get together and exclude a child while spreading gossip about her. The difference is that the scope of influence has expanded, and a beast has been unleashed. Whereas most children can handle being excluded or teased at school, the enormity of the broadcast on the Internet is too much for some to bear. So what might begin as innocent gossip can mutate into rumors that can turn into cyber-bullying, and there is a lack of clear rules about how to control this new beast.

Parents need to discuss some of these issues with their children, particularly if their children are naïve and perhaps more vulnerable to people who might pose as their friends. In this chapter, I encourage parents to make sure they define privacy rules with their children and also make agreements about what should be spread on the Internet. We also revisit some old etiquette rules and suggest that they may have new applications in this world of technology and cyberspace.

10.1   Cell Phone Etiquette and Rules

If the child is not good at reading STOP signs or knowing when he or she is bothering someone else, then he or she will need clear rules about when and where to use a cell phone. To avoid ambiguity, teach specific rules for specific situations.

Discuss the basics first:

- Don't talk on the phone at a restaurant. If you get a call, excuse yourself and go outside.
- Don't text at the table while eating with others. They will see it as rude because it appears that whoever is on the phone is more important to you than they are.
- Turn off your phone when you are in a movie house, theater, or a music or lecture hall.

Other Cell Phone Rules

- If you are eating in a restaurant, if you have to take the call, step outside.
- If your school allows cell phone use during breaks, then it is OK to use one. See if you can step away from other children who might not wish to hear your conversation.
- Turn your phone off or to vibrate during an after-school activity. If you have to take a call, step away from the other children or go outside.
- While traveling on the bus, if cell phone use is allowed, use texting. Think about the other passengers: do you really want them to hear your conversation? They probably would like it if you kept it between the two of you.
- When you are a guest at someone else's house, the same rules apply as in a restaurant. If you have to take a call, go into another room and be brief. Unless you involve the hosting child in the conversation, you are being rude, giving him the message that the child on the phone is more important than he is.
- When having a friend over at your house, the same rules apply as those in the previous point. If you must take the call, do, but it is best to tell the person that you will call him or her later, after your friend leaves. When you are with a friend but take a call from another person, the meta-message is that the person on the phone is more important.

The Meta-Message and Cell Phone Use

The unspoken message you give to the person you are with when you take a cell phone call from someone else is that the person on the phone is more important to you than the person in front of you.

10.2　Rules About Internet Use

Note: This section is intended for parents.

Parents need to be aware of their children's use of the Internet. Children from eight to eighteen years of age spend hours a day communicating in a virtual world. Whether they are on MySpace or Facebook (or other social networking sites), in chat rooms, or using instant messaging (IM), they communicate with others using the Web to socialize, set up dates, and experiment with their identity. Their use of cyberspace is unprecedented.

Parents need to be clear to their children about what information should not be shared in cyberspace for privacy and safety reasons. Some parents do not let their children use the Internet for social purposes because they don't trust their children's judgment or think that their children's safety might be compromised. Because the Internet is here to stay, however, and is a great way to connect with people around the world who share similar interests or who have similar issues or problems, it is important to impart some safety rules for children. This is a good time to review Exercise 4: Private or Public Talk? referring to this box.

What You Don't Want Your Child to Post on the Web

- Identity information (for example, phone numbers)
- Unflattering pictures of anyone
- Pictures of anyone else without that person's permission
- Private information about anyone
- Taboo topics (anything that involves violence or sex or that is illegal)
- Private thoughts or fears
- Personal family problems
- Sexual experiences or issues

Parents need to give their children a clear message about what information is supposed to be private—for example, addresses, phone numbers, the name of their school, or where their after-school activities are—and that it should only be shared with friends, *not* broadcast on their wall for everyone who is in their network to see. Although most of the people using Facebook and MySpace are not harmful, there are

Private information includes where you live, where you go to school, and where you will be after school.

people who use them to try to meet young boys and girls. Discuss the difference between posting a picture of an event after it happened and tagging their friends (sending it to them) versus posting information on their wall.

10.3　Cyber-Bullying

Along with the increased use of cyberspace, there is a new form of bullying, perhaps more powerful than the old form because the perpetrator may or may not be identified and the scope of influence is potentially much larger than the crowd a bully on the playground gathers. The idea that "everyone" knows has a greater psychological impact on the child.

Cyber-bullying, as defined by cyber-psychology expert Dr. Larry Rosen (2007), includes

- Sending unwanted, mean, vulgar, or threatening e-mails, text messages, or IMs
- Posting sensitive or private information about someone on the Internet
- Altering photos and posting them on a Web site
- Sending or spreading gossip or rumors online
- Impersonating another person (creating a phony MySpace page, for example) and posting information to make someone look bad

The two factors that make this form of teasing or bullying dangerous are that the perpetrator can be disguised or unknown and that the number of people who can get drawn into the circle of perpetrator and victim is huge. Children used to be able to go home and escape teasing. Internet bullying stays with the child 24/7. It is important for parents to have open communication with their children so that the children will share any of their concerns. Some of these children might be tempted to be the perpetrators of bullying as well; this is another reason to have clear rules about Internet use.

Parents and teachers should report to the appropriate legal authorities any bullying or discussion of suicide or threats to another.

There are numerous Web sites with good advice on cyber-bullying.

Exercise 36: Watch "Kids Online"

Note: Although teachers can show this video as a classroom exercise, this is intended as an activity for parents and their children.

Make a date to watch this PBS show, produced by *Frontline,* with your child. This documentary, which originally aired January 20, 2008, can be viewed on the PBS Web site: www.pbs.org/wgbh/pages/frontline/kidsonline. It is a disturbing examination of a young girl's suicide that was directly related to cyber-bullying.

Discuss the impact of cyber-bullying on your child and ask him to share any examples of situations that are similar.

Make a deal with your child that she will keep you (or someone at school) informed if she becomes aware of anyone doing this type of bullying. Also make it clear that you want to be informed if she sees any threats on the Internet to anyone she knows or if she reads or sees anything that indicates someone is considering suicide or any type of crime.

Conclusion: Learning Social Skills Is a Lifelong Process

Children who have trouble processing information will need more repetition to learn all of the social skills. They will need to practice them throughout their childhood. As they learn to evaluate their own behavior more effectively, they will increase their learning of social skills. The goal of *Socially ADDept* is to aid parents, family members, teachers, and other school personnel in breaking social skills down into their fundamental pieces so that it will be easier for children with SN to assimilate them.

Due to the complex nature of social skills, it will take time to learn and use these skills. Perseveration, failing to show interest, being pushy, failing to comprehend and use tone and body language appropriately, and failing to check when mind reading are habitual behaviors that will take time to change. These habits need to be unlearned and replaced with the new skills. It should not be expected that children will acquire them quickly. The pragmatics of communication and mind reading often baffle sophisticated adults, not to mention children. Interpersonal dynamics operate in a fluid medium and are constantly changing as new input is received, which requires flexibility and good mind-reading skills.

The goal is for children to acquire a new mindfulness and a greater ability to self-reflect. Using the self-evaluation forms and the feedback methods suggested, teachers and parents work with the children to acquire better self-monitoring skills. As explained, when adults verify with children that their perception is correct, it helps children start to see their interactions the way others might see them (joint perception). Because this involves a shift in their frames of reference, children often start to observe how their behavior affects others, which is a huge development for many of these children. This ability to see events from another person's point of view is fundamental to be able to mind-read successfully.

The meta-goal of *Socially ADDept* has been to make the acquisition of complex skills seem simple. It is my hope that by simplifying complex skills and breaking them into smaller, incremental steps, this book offers children, parents, teachers, and other professionals a better road map of the terrain and more tools for their toolbox.

Part III

Appendices

What Is ADHD?

Attention Deficit Hyperactivity Disorder (ADHD) is most often an organic problem. It is characterized by the inability to sustain focused attention (distractibility or inattention). To diagnose ADHD, mental health professionals ask parents and teachers to observe the child and rate his or her behavior using specific questionnaires or checklists. These checklists rate the following behaviors, which are present in most people with ADHD:

- Distractibility
- Inattention
- Free flight of ideas (free associations to any other idea)
- Impulsivity—moodiness
- Insatiability
- Bursts of hot temper
- Hyperactivity

In most cases, these behaviors are noticed before the child is seven years old. Because the ability of a person with ADHD to stay focused gets worse when the environment is noisy or full of distractions, teachers often are the first ones to notice when children are having trouble paying attention.

There are two major subtypes: ADHD with hyperactivity and ADHD without hyperactivity (inattentive form).

ADHD with hyperactivity is often easier to diagnose, as these children move continuously, have trouble sitting still, have poor impulse control, and may have temper outbursts more frequently than their peers.

Whereas the hyperactive child with ADHD is obvious to any experienced teacher, the child with ADHD, inattentive form, may get overlooked. Professionals now believe that the comorbidity of learning disabilities and ADHD, inattentive form, may be as high as 50 percent. This subgroup is not as easy to diagnose because they may not create as much trouble as children with hyperactivity. Instead of creating problems, they may just appear spaced out or unfocused. This children may demonstrate excessive anxiety or shyness, and they be poor academic achievers. Often missed are girls and children who come from lower socioeconomic communities or who are nonnative English speakers; the assumption is often that their learning or social problems are emotional in nature or due to lower intelligence or motivation stemming from socioeconomic or family problems.

The mixed group can include children who have a comorbid diagnosis of oppositional-defiant disorder (OCD). This group of children can exhibit more aggressive behaviors and consequently can experience social rejection for failing to follow rules or being disruptive. They often fall in with others who have aggression issues. This subgroup is at risk for breaking rules, intruding, and even engaging in criminal activities. (More children with comorbid ADHD and oppositional-defiant disorder get in trouble with the law, are incarcerated, or become addicted to drugs or alcohol.)

How ADHD Affects the Brain

Simply stated, the brains of individuals with ADHD function differently; the frontal cortex functions more slowly, and less glucose is metabolized in the prefrontal cortex. One way to describe this is that the executive functions of the brain process sensory information too slowly. This means that the person fails to sort and store sensory stimuli. When the stimulation level is low, the person can focus well, even hyperfocus. But put the same person in a room filled with noise or activity, and he or she becomes overstimulated by the amount of sensory information. The person is unable to filter it out or process it fast enough.

New research indicates that this failure to limit or store sensory information may be due to increased levels of dopamine in the caudate, an area of the brain that is responsible for putting on the brain's "brakes." This increase of dopamine is thought to slow down the braking mechanism.

Is ADHD a Learning Disability?

It is clear that having ADHD can affect a child's ability to learn in a highly stimulating environment, such as a noisy classroom, due to the amount of auditory and visual distractions. However, ADHD is not a learning disability per se. If the child functions at least one-and-a-half to two years below grade level as the result of ADHD, the same criteria for services apply as for children with learning disabilities (meaning he or she is eligible for special services under IDEA). One reason people think ADHD is a learning disability is that many children and adults have a learning disability along with their ADHD.

Evaluation for ADHD

1. **History.** A health professional should take a comprehensive family history. It needs to include when someone first noticed a problem. Because assessment is based on the presence of these symptoms before the age of seven, particular attention needs to be paid to children's preschool and early elementary school experiences.

2. **Identification of other family members with ADHD.**
   - Does a parent, sibling, aunt, uncle, cousin, or grandparent have ADHD?
   - Did this relative have an inconsistent job history?
   - Did this person have problems with his or her temper?
   - Was the relative or dependent on drugs or alcohol?

3. **Behavior checklists.** After consulting a medical doctor or psychologist, the parent and the classroom teacher(s) are asked to fill out behavior checklists. These are standardized lists that look for typical ADHD behaviors. Sometimes achievement tests are used in addition to checklists.

4. **Psychological tests** are sometimes used to define the scope of the problem. Because they can be costly, they are not always used.

5. **Medication trials.** One way of defining the presence of ADHD is to see if a trial of medication gets rid of the major symptoms. Many children experience an immediate change in impulsivity, hyperactivity, or moodiness. Medication trials are regulated by medical doctors.

6. **Continuous performance tests.** IVA and TOVA are computerized tests that are popular means of assessment. Although the creators of the tests say they aren't to be used as a sole means of assessing ADHD, many clinicians are using them in this way.

   Note: Continuous performance tests are not as valid if the child has eye-hand coordination problems (caused by a learning disability).

   A positive use for these tests is to demonstrate increased attention or shorter response time. In other words, children should take the test before starting a treatment regime and then take it again after their treatments and compare the results.

Warning

Do not diagnose yourself or your child. See a competent medical doctor, psychologist, school psychologist, or psychotherapist who is familiar with ADHD. Children and Adults with Attention Deficit Hyperactivity Disorder (CHADD) is an international support group and a good resource for finding other parents and professionals who work well with this population.

What Are Learning Disabilities?

Most learning disabilities are thought to be genetic, and they often run in families. Researchers have actually autopsied dyslexic brains and have found some anatomical differences that suggest why people with learning disabilities process information differently.[1]

The most common learning disability is dyslexia, a disorder that affects a person's ability to see and comprehend written symbols.[2] But all learning disabilities affect how information is processed, stored, or retrieved and can be specific to any symbol system (such as mathematics or writing). Disabilities can also affect the retrieval of learned information, which is very distressing to children and adults who know they know the material but are unable to demonstrate it while being tested.

Dyslexia (*dys,* "cannot"; *lexia,* "words") affects how well the child can read, write, and spell. The other kinds of learning disabilities affect

- Speech (aphasia)
- Reading (dyslexia)
- Writing (dysgraphia)
- Mathematics (dyscalcula)
- Hearing (auditory processing deficit)
- Memory (short- and long-term retrieval problems)
- Coordination (apraxia)
- Nonverbal expressions and comprehension (NLD)

Learning disabilities can affect all aspects of how any information is acquired, processed, retrieved, or communicated. A Nonverbal Learning Disability (NLD) affects how well a person can communicate nonverbally and understand the meaning of others' use of nonverbal body language. (More than 60 percent of any communication is nonverbal and supplies the context to understand the spoken words.)

An important part of the definition put forth by the National Joint Committee on Learning Disabilities (1991) is that learning disabilities are "significant difficulties in the acquisition and use of listening, speaking, reading, writing, reasoning, or mathematical abilities. These disorders are intrinsic to the individual and presumed due to central nervous system dysfunction."

If your child is functioning one to two years below grade level, you can request that he or she be tested for learning disabilities by your local public school (even if your child does not attend that school). You need to submit the request in writing. All children with learning disabilities are entitled to remedial help under Federal Law 94-142 (IDEA), which also requires your local public school to test children to see if they qualify for services.

Possible school-based services can include

- Tutoring (in class or in a pull-out program) with reading, spelling, writing, or math
- Speech therapy
- Adaptive physical education
- Psychological counseling
- Classroom accommodations
- Use of assistive technology
- Audiobooks or digital books that can be used in a reader with auditory and visual feedback
- Programs that teach auditory skills
- Social skills training

After the testing is completed, a meeting should be arranged with the parent or guardian, school psychologist, teacher, associate principal, and resource personnel. The purpose of this meeting is for the school to define the course of action it plans to take to help your child master his or her deficiencies. It should include a summary of his or her test results, annual goals, and a description of the services (tutoring, speech therapy, adaptive physical education, and so on) that the school plans to provide.

Evaluation for Learning Disabilities

Testing for learning problems is usually done by a psychologist.[3] Children are tested for IQ (if allowed in your state) or ability using other performance tests. Their ability is compared with their academic performance. When a child performs at least one-and-a-half years below his or her ability, and there is no other emotional or psychological cause that explains this lack of performance, he or she can be referred to testing for specific learning disabilities. The tests can include

- Standard achievement tests
- IQ or performance tests
- Specific tests to measure reading, writing, mathematics, speech, auditory sequencing, visual, or motor skills, social skills, and memory

Children who have severe learning disabilities can be evaluated in preschool, but are most commonly evaluated during the first three years of elementary school.

School districts often focus on children who are performing below grade level (with boys being diagnosed more frequently than girls). Children who come from disadvantaged backgrounds are often not properly assessed, for two reasons: (1) a professional also has to observe that the child has an innate ability that is not being manifested, and (2) this lack of achievement cannot result from a psychological issue, such as lack of motivation or emotional problems due to abuse or neglect.

Notes

1. MRI studies suggest that there are actually changes within the neuronal structure of autopsied dyslexic brains that indicate a different neuronal structure (Hugadahl, 1993). One idea is that there may be a lack of brain dominance; Galaburda (1993) found that 20 percent of dyslexics had symmetry in the language regions of the brain instead of the usual one-sided brain dominance. This observation may suggest that there too many signals and a lack of a clear command center (Caviness, Filipek, & Kennedy, 1993).

2. Fifty years ago, the term *dyslexia* covered the largest group of people thought to have learning disabilities. With more accurate diagnosis and descriptions, the diagnostic terms more accurately describe the condition (even if they confuse the parents). Most people with learning disabilities are dyslexic and most have auditory sequencing problems. Manis (1994) suggests that this disability is stable over time.

3. The diagnosis of a specific learning disability is based on a discrepancy score: ability − performance = 1.5 standard deviations below ability or grade level. The lack of performance cannot be attributed to any environmental, social, or psychological factor.

What Is Asperger's Syndrome?

Asperger's Syndrome (AS) is the official name of a relatively new diagnosis (American Psychiatric Association, 1994) describing a person who functions on the high end of Autism Spectrum Disorders (ASD). People who have AS have above-average intelligence and can function well academically and even professionally but have extreme social problems that manifest as poor social skills and an inability to process nonverbal body language. Some have flat or atonal speech or use odd, repetitive motions or gestures.[1]

Most children with AS and ASD benefit from early diagnosis. Researchers have found that children make huge gains when treatment is started before the age of two. Several researchers (Mundy, Sigman, & Kasari, 1990; Mundy & Crowson, 1997; Whalen & Schreibman, 2003) have concluded that children who learn joint attention (increased pointing and sharing of events or objects, showing toys, or looking at the other person while inspecting a new object) make significant gains in their language abilities. This is important because children who do not develop language skills (talking before age five or six) are more likely to have trouble developing peer relationships (also see note 6 in Chapter One).

A recent study conducted by researchers at the University of Nottingham found that children with AS can learn to recognize facial expressions, particularly eye expressions, when the faces are animated (Back, Ropar, & Mitchell, 2007). Other studies suggest that children with AS may avoid social interactions and may have social anxiety.

A unique characteristic of people with AS is that they often have repetitive mannerisms, such as holding their body in a rigid way; their posture or motions seem stilted or inflexible; or they may use repetitive motions. Many speak in a robotic manner without using normal variations in their tone. Because they may lack inflection in their tone, they may also have difficulty comprehending the emotional meanings that tones convey.

Children with AS often perseverate (talk at length and in great detail on topics that they find interesting), and they may be unaware that the other person is uninterested. They often have obsessive routines and may be preoccupied with a particular subject of interest. They have a great deal of difficulty reading nonverbal cues (body language) and very often have difficulty determining proper body space. They may be overly sensitive to sounds, tastes, smells, and sights. Their behaviors are due to neurological differences and not the result of intentional rudeness and most certainly not the result of "improper parenting."

AS is a neurobiological disorder named for a Viennese physician, Hans Asperger, who in 1944 published a paper that described a pattern of behaviors in several young boys who had normal intelligence and language development, but who also exhibited autistic-like behaviors and marked deficiencies in social and communication skills. It wasn't until 1994 that AS was added to the *Diagnostic and Statistical Manual of Mental Disorders, Fourth Edition (DSM-IV)*, and only in the past few years has AS been recognized by professionals and parents. The total number of children with ASD has increased tenfold over the last decade. A recent report suggested that there has been an increase in the diagnosis from 1 in 300 children to 1 in 150. No cause has yet been associated with the increase.[2]

The following are the diagnostic criteria for Asperger's Syndrome, adapted from the *DSM-IV* (American Psychiatric Society, 1994):[3]

A. Qualitative impairment in social interaction, as manifested by at least two of the following:

  1. Marked impairments in the use of multiple nonverbal behaviors, such as eye-to-eye gaze, facial expression, body postures, and gestures to regulate social interaction

  2. Failure to develop peer relationships appropriate to developmental level

  3. A lack of spontaneous seeking to share enjoyment, interests, or achievements with other people (for example, by a lack of showing, bringing, or pointing out objects of interest to other people)

  4. Lack of social or emotional reciprocity

B. Restricted repetitive and stereotyped patterns of behavior, interests, and activities, as manifested by at least one of the following:

  1. Encompassing preoccupation with one or more stereotyped and restricted patterns of interest that is abnormal either in intensity or focus

2. Apparently inflexible adherence to specific, nonfunctional routines or rituals

3. Stereotyped and repetitive motor mannerisms (for example, hand or finger flapping or twisting, or complex whole-body movements)

4. Persistent preoccupation with parts of objects

Notes

1. AS is characterized by atonal speech and rigid body language or the use of repetitive gestures, which are not present in people with Nonverbal Learning Disability (NLD). The disorders are similar in that individuals with these disabilities share a difficulty with understanding and using nonverbal body language appropriately. They both fail to learn social rules; however, the effects of NLD are not as pervasive as those of AS.

2. Dr. Hollander at Mt. Sinai had been engaged in a study that examined the occurrence of autism among children whose mothers had received pitocin at birth (to speed up delivery, a practice used in about 25 percent of U.S. births). One theory of the research was that pitocin was somehow replacing oxytocin (the bonding hormone that controls lactation in women) in the brains of the young infants. Hollander's newest work (Hollander et al., 2003) uses oxytocin to reduce repetitive behaviors in adults with autism and Asperger's Syndrome.

3. It has been proposed that the next edition of the *DSM* would eliminate Asperger's Syndrome as a separate diagnosis and fold it back in to the diagnosis of ASD. The major difference would be that it would lose the distinction of its unique characteristics of high intelligence combined with autism. Some feel it would have repercussions for therapeutic reimbursement or attach a more negative stigma to those with the diagnosis. This alteration in diagnostic coding is not being well received by people with Asperger's Syndrome or the supporting therapeutic community.

Bibliography
and Resources

Bibliography

Achenbach, T., & Edelbrock, C. (1983). *Manual for the Child Behavior Checklist and Revised Child Behavior Profile*. Burlington: University of Vermont.

American Psychiatric Association. (1994). *Diagnostic and Statistical Manual of Mental Disorders, Fourth Edition*. Washington, DC: Author.

Armstrong, T. (1987). *In their own way: Discovering and encouraging your child's personal learning style*. New York: Putnam.

Attwood, T. (2007). *The complete guide to Asperger's Syndrome*. London: Kingsley.

Ayers, A. J. (1972). *Sensory integration and learning disorders*. Los Angeles: Western Psychological Services.

Back, E., Ropar, D., & Mitchell, P. (2007, March-April). Do the eyes have it? Inferring mental states from animated faces in autism. *Journal of Child Development, 78*, 397–411.

Baker, J. (2003). *Social skills training for children and adolescents with Asperger's Syndrome and social-communication problems*. Shawnee Mission, KS: Autism Asperger Publishing.

Baker, J. (2006). *Social skills picture book for high school and beyond*. Shawnee Mission, KS: Autism Asperger Publishing.

Barkley, R. A. (1990). *Attention Deficit Hyperactivity Disorder: A handbook for diagnosis and treatment*. New York: Guildford Press.

Baron-Cohen, S. (2009). *Mind reading: The interactive guide to emotions, Version 1.3*. [CD-ROM]. London: Kingsley.

Bateson, G. (1972). *Steps to an ecology of mind: Collected essays in anthropology, psychiatry, evolution, and epistemology*. Chicago: University of Chicago Press.

Berne, E. (1964). *Games people play*. New York: Ballantine Books.

Biederman, J. (2003). Pharmacotherapy for attention-deficit/hyperactivity disorder (ADHD) decreases the risk for substance abuse: Findings from a longitudinal follow-up of youths with and without ADHD. *Journal of Clinical Psychiatry, 64*(suppl. 11), 3–8. www.psychiatrist.com/pcc/pcpdf/v05s05/v64s1101.pdf.

Biederman, J., Munir, K., & Knee, D. (1987). Conduct and oppositional disorder in clinically referred children with attention deficit disorder: A controlled family study. *Journal of the Academy of Child and Adolescent Psychiatry, 26*, 724–727.

Biederman, J., Wilens, T., Mick, E., Spencer, T., & Faraone, S. (1999). Pharmacotherapy of attention-deficit/hyperactivity disorder reduces risk for substance use. *Pediatrics*, http:pediatrics.aappublications.org/cgi/content/abstract/104/2/.

Bierman, K. L., & Wargo, J. B. (1995). Predicting the longitudinal course associated with aggressive-rejected, aggressive (nonrejected) and rejected (nonaggressive) status. *Development and Psychopathology, 7*, 669–682.

Bloomquist, M. L. (1996). *Skills training for children with behavior disorders: A parent and therapist guidebook*. New York: Guildford Press.

Bollinger, C. (n.d.). *My turn, your turn: Songs for building social skills*. Available as CD or downloadable file at www.songsforteaching.com/index/html.

Borenstein, S., & Radman, Z. (1984). *Learning to learn: An approach to study skills*. Dubuque, IO: Kendall/Hunt.

Brooks, R., & Goldstein, S. (2002). *Raising resilient children: Fostering strength, hope, and optimism in your child*. Baltimore: Brookes.

Buron, K. D., & Curtis, M. (2003). *Incredible 5 point scale*. Shawnee Mission, KS: Autism Asperger Publishing.

Caviness, V. S., Filipek, P. A., & Kennedy, D. N. (1993). The neurobiology of learning disabilities: Potential contributions from magnetic resonance imaging. In A. M. Galaburda (Ed.), *Dyslexia and development: Neurobiological aspects of extra-ordinary brains*. Cambridge, MA: President and the Fellows of Harvard College. (257–296.)

Chodorow, N. (1978). *The reproduction of mothering*. Berkeley: University of California Press.

Cohen-Posey, K. (1995). *How to handle bullies, teasers and other meanies*. Highland City, FL: Rainbow Books.

Community Alliance for Special Education and Protection and Advocacy. (1994). *Special education rights and responsibilities*. San Francisco: Author. Available at www.caseadvocacy.org/handbook.html.

Cowley, G., "Understanding Autism." *Newsweek*, July 31, 2000. Available at http://www .newsweek.com/2000/07/30/understanding-autism/html

Cowen, E. L., Pederson, A., Babigan, H., Izzo, I. D., & Trost, M. A. (1973). Long term follow-up of early detected vulnerable children. *Journal of Consulting and Clinical Psychology, 41*, 438–446.

Cratty, B. (1996). Coordination problems among learning disabled children: Meanings and implications. In B. Cratty & R. L. Goldman (Eds.), *Learning disabilities: Contemporary viewpoints*. Amsterdam: Harwood Academic. (141–185.)

Curran, S., & Fitzgerald, M. (1999). Attention Deficit Hyperactivity Disorder in the prison population. *American Journal of Psychology, 156*, 1664–1665.

Davis, L., Sirotowitz, S., & Parker, H. C. (1996). *Study strategies made easy: A practical plan for school success*. Plantation, FL: Specialty Press.

De Shazer, S. (1991). *Putting difference to work*. New York: Norton.

Dockstader, M., & Payne, L. (1989). *To a different drummer: Helping children with learning disabilities*. Albuquerque, NM: ISS Publications.

Erikson, E. (1968). *Identity: Youth and crisis*. New York: Norton.

Evangelista, N. M. (2009). *An examination of the self-protective hypothesis in children with ADHD: The role of achievement*. Unpublished doctoral thesis, Ohio University.

Evans-Morris, S., Lande, A., & Wiz, B. (1998). *Marvelous mouth music: Songs for speech therapy and beyond*. [CD-ROM/booklet]. Boulder, CO: Belle Curve Records.

Everett, C. A., & Volgy-Everett, S. (1999). *Family therapy for ADHD: Treating children, adolescents and adults*. New York: Guilford Press.

Faraone, S.V., Biederman, J., Mick, E., Williamson, S., Wilens, T., Spencer, T., Weber, W., Jetton, J., Kraus, I., Pert, J., & Zallen, B. (2000). Family study of girls with ADHD. *American Journal of Psychiatry, 157*, 1077–1083.

Fox, C. L., & Weaver, F. (1989, July). Social acceptance of students identified as learning disabled. *Journal of Teacher Education, 12*(3): 83–90.

Frankel, F. (1996). *Good friends are hard to find: Help your child find, make and keep friends*. Glendale, CA: Perspective.

Frankel, F., & Myatt, R. (2003). *Children's friendship training*. New York: Brunner-Routledge.

Gabor, D. (1983). *How to start a conversation and make friends*. New York: Simon & Schuster.

Bibliography and Resources

Galaburda, A. M. (1993). (Ed.). *Dyslexia and development: Neurobiological aspects of extra-ordinary brains*. Cambridge, MA: President and the Fellows of Harvard College.

Garrity, C., Jens, K., Porter, W., Sager, N., & Short-Camilli, C. (2000). *Bully-proofing your school: A comprehensive approach for elementary schools* (2nd ed.). Longmont, CO: Sopris West.

Giler, J. Z. (1998a). *ADDept Social Skills Curriculum: A ten week curriculum to teach 10 basic social skills and self evaluation to children with ADHD/LD problems*. Santa Barbara, CA: Author.

Giler, J. Z. (1998b). *From acting out to fitting in*. [DVD]. Santa Barbara, CA: Karl L. Metzenberg.

Giler, J. Z. (1999, August-September). ADHD: What every therapist needs to know. *Family Therapy News, 30*(4), 22.

Giler, 2000 *Socially ADDEpt: A Manual for Parents whose children have ADHD and or Learning Disabilities*. CES Santa Barbara, CA.

Giler, J. Z. (2001). Are girls with ADHD socially adept? *California Biofeedback, 17*(2), http://www.biofeedbackcalifornia.org/Uploads/Past_Issues/BSC_Spring_2001.pdf.

Giler, J. Z. (2002). Helping kids with learning disabilities understand the language of friendship. GreatSchools. http://www.greatschools.org/special-education/health/understanding-the-language-of-friendship.gs?content=805.

Gilligan, C. (1974). *In a different voice*. Cambridge, MA: Harvard University Press.

Goldstein, A. (1988). *The Prepare Curriculum: Teaching prosocial competencies*. Champaign, IL: Research Press.

Goldstein, S. (1996). *Managing attention and learning disorders in late adolescence and adulthood: A guide for practitioners*. Hoboken, NJ: Wiley.

Goleman, D. (1993). *Emotional intelligence: Why it can matter more than IQ*. New York: Bantam Books.

Gray, C. (1994). *Comic strip conversations*. Jenison, MI: Jenison Public Schools.

Greene, R. W. (1998). *The explosive child: A new approach for understanding and parenting easily frustrated, "chronically inflexible" children*. New York: HarperCollins.

Gresham, F. M. (1982). Misguided mainstreaming: The case for social skills training with handicapped children. *Teaching Exceptional Children, 48*, 422–433. Reston, VA: Council for Exceptional Children.

Gresham, F. M. (1982). *Social skills: Principles, practices and procedures*. Des Moines: Iowa Department of Public Instruction.

Gresham, F. M. (1990). Best practices in social skills training. In A. Thomas & J. Grimes (Eds.), *Best practices in school psychology II* (pp. 695–709). Washington, DC: National Association of School Psychologists.

Gresham, F. M., & Elliott, S. N. (1994). *Social Skills Rating System (parent, teacher and student forms and manual)*. Circle Pines: MN: American Guidance Service.

Guevremont, D. (1990). Social skills and peer relationship training. In R. A. Barclay (Ed.), *Attention-Deficit Hyperactivity Disorder: A handbook for diagnosis and treatment*. New York: Guilford Press.

Hallowell, E. M., & Ratey, J. (1994). *Driven to distraction*. New York: Simon & Schuster.

Hollander, E., Novotny, S., Hanratty, M., Yaffe, R., DeCaria, C., Aronowitz, C., & Mosovich, S. (2003). Oxytocin infusion reduces repetitive behaviors in adults with autistic and Asperger's disorders. *Neuropsychopharmacology, 28*, 193–198.

Howlin, P., Baron-Cohen, S., & Hadwin, J. (1999). *Teaching children with autism to mind-read: A practical guide*. Hoboken, NJ: Wiley.

Hoza, B., Pelham, W. E., Dobbs, J., Owens, J. S., & Pillow, D. R. (2002). Do boys with Attention-Deficit/Hyperactivity Disorder have positive illusory self-concepts? *Journal of Abnormal Psychology, 111*, 268–278.

Hugadahl, K. (1993). Functional brain asymmetry, dyslexia and immune disorders. In A. M. Galaburda (Ed.), *Dyslexia and development: Neurobiological aspects of extra-ordinary brains*. Cambridge, MA: President and the Fellows of Harvard College.

Ingersoll, B., & Goldstein, S. (1995). *Lonely, sad and angry: A parent's guide to depression in children and adolescents*. New York: Doubleday.

Kasari, C., Paperella, T., Freeman, S., & Jahromi, L. B. (2008). Language outcome in autism: Randomized comparison of joint attention and play interventions. *Journal of Consulting and Clinical Psychology, 76*, 125–137.

Kelly, K., & Ramundo, P. (1993). *You mean I'm not lazy, stupid or crazy?* New York: Scribner.

Klin, A., & Volkmar, F. (1995). *Asperger's Syndrome: Guidelines for assessment and diagnosis*. Pittsburgh, PA: Learning Disabilities Association of America. http://childstudycenter .yale.edu/autism/Images/asdiagnosis_tcm339-34860.pdf.

Kline, F. M., & Silver, L. B. (Eds.). (2004). *The educator's guide to mental health issues in the classroom*. Baltimore: Brookes.

Koegel, R., & Koegel, L. (2009). *Pivotal response treatments for autism: Communication, social and academic development*. Baltimore: Brookes.

Lande, A. (1999). *Song games for sensory integration*. Boulder, CO: Belle Curve Records.

Lara, J. (2009). *Aut-erobic: Autism movement therapy* [DVD]. Culver City, CA: Autism Movement Therapy.

Laugeson, E. A., Frankel, F., Mogil, C., & Dillon, A. R. (2009). Parent-assisted social skills training to improve friendships in teens with autism spectrum disorders. *Journal of Autism and Developmental Disorders, 39*, 596–606.

Laugeson, E. A., & Frankel, F. (2010). *Social skills for teenagers with developmental and autism spectrum disorders: The PEERS treatment manual*. New York: Brunner-Routledge.

Lavoie, R. (1985). *How difficult can this be? The F.A.T. City Workshop*. [DVD]. Washington, DC: Public Broadcasting System.

Lavoie, R. (1994). *Last one picked, first one picked on*. [DVD]. Washington, DC: Public Broadcasting System.

Lavoie, R. (2005). *It's so much work to be your friend: Helping the child with learning disabilities find social success*. New York: Simon & Schuster.

Lord, C., Rutter, M., DiLavore, P. C., & Risi, S. (2002). *Autism Diagnostic Observation Schedule*. Los Angeles, CA: Western Psychological Services.

Lord, C., Risi, S., Lambrecht, L., Cook, E. H., Jr., Leventhal, B. L., DiLavore, P. C., Pickles, A., & Rutter, M. (2000). Autism Diagnostic Observation Schedule - Generic: A standard measure of social and communication deficits associated with the spectrum of autism. *Journal of Autism & Developmental Disorders, 30*(3), 205–223.

McGinnis, E., Goldstein, A., Sprafkin, R. P., & Gershaw, N. J. (1984). *Skillstreaming the elementary school child*. Champaign, IL: Research Press Company.

Maccoby, E. E. (1988). Gender as a social category. *Developmental Psychology, 24*, 755–765.

Maccoby, E. E. (1990). Gender and relationships: A developmental account. *American Psychologist, 45*, 513–520.

Maccoby, E. E., & Jacklin, C. N. (1974). *The psychology of sex differences*. Stanford, CA: Stanford University Press.

Maedgen, J. W. (2000). Social functioning and emotional regulation in the Attention Deficit Hyperactivity Disorder subtypes. *Journal of Clinical Child Psychology, 29*, 30–42.

Manis, F. (1996). Current trends in dyslexia research. In B. Cratty & R. L. Goldman (Eds.), *Learning disabilities: Contemporary viewpoints*. Amsterdam: Harwood Academic, 27–42.

Mannuzza, S., Klein, R. G., Konig, P. H., & Giampino, T. L. (1989). Hyperactive boys almost grown up, IV: Criminality and its relationship to psychiatric status. *Archives of General Psychiatry, 46*, 1073–1079.

MTA Cooperative Group. (1999). A 14-month randomized clinical trial of treatment strategies for attention-deficit/hyperactivity disorder (ADHD). *Archives of General Psychiatry, 56*, 1073–1086.

Mundy, P., & Crowson, M. (1997). Joint attention and early social communication: Implications for research on intervention in autism. *Development and Psychopathology, 7*, 63–82.

Mundy, P., Gwaltney, M., & Henderson, H. (2010). Self referenced processing, neural development, and joint attention in autism. *Journal of Autism, 14*(4), 1–22.

Mundy, P., Sigman, M., & Kasari, C. (1990). A longitudinal study of joint attention and language development in autistic children. *Journal of Autism and Developmental Disorders, 20*, 115–128.

Myles, B. S., & Southwick, J. (2005). *Asperger's Syndrome and difficult moments: Practical solutions for tantrums, rage and meltdowns* (2nd ed.). Shawnee, KS: Autism Asperger Publishing.

Nadeau, K. (1994). *Survival guide for college students with ADD or LD*. Washington, DC: Magination Press.

Nadeau, K., Littman, E., & Quinn, P. (1999). *Understanding girls with AD/HD*. Silver Springs, MD: Advantage Books.

National Joint Committee on Learning Disabilities. (1991). Learning disabilities: Issues on definition. *Asha, 33*(suppl. 5), 18–20.

Norwicki, S., & Duke, M. (1992). *Helping the child who doesn't fit in*. Atlanta: Peachtree.

Novotni, M. (1999). *What does everyone else know that I don't? Social skills help for adults with ADHD*. Plantation, FL: Specialty Press.

Ohan, J. L., & Johnston, C. (2002). Are the performance overestimates given by boys with ADHD self-protective? *Journal of Clinical Child Psychology*, 31, 230–241.

Owens, J. S., Goldfine, M. E., Evangelista, N. M., Hoza, B., & Kaiser, N. M. (2007). A critical review of self-perceptions and the positive illusory bias in children with ADHD. *Clinical Child and Family Psychology Review, 10*, 335–351.

Parker, H. C. (1996). *Behavior management at home: A token economy program for children and teens*. Plantation, FL: Specialty Press.

Phelan, T. W. (1993). *Surviving your adolescents: A vital parents' guide*. Glen Ellyn, IL: Parent Magic. (Also available as a DVD and in Spanish.)

Phelan, T. W. (2003). *1,2,3 magic: Effective discipline for children 2–12*. Glen Ellyn, IL: Parent Magic.

Rief, S. F. (2005). *How to reach and teach children with ADD/ADHD: Practical techniques, strategies and interventions for helping children with attention problems and hyperactivity* (2nd ed.). San Francisco: Jossey-Bass.

Roberts, C. A., & Elliott, P. T. (1995). *ADHD and teens*. Dallas, TX: Taylor.

Robinson, J. E. (2007). *Look me in the eye: My life with Asperger's*. New York: Three Rivers Press.

Rosen, L. D. (2007). *Me, My Space, and I: Parenting the net generation*. New York: Palgrave Macmillan.

Rosenholtz, S. (1993). *Move like the animals*. New York: Feldenkrais Institute. (Also available as a video and DVD.)

Rubin, K. (2002). *The friendship factor*. New York: Penguin Books.

Shaywitz, S. (2003). *Overcoming dyslexia: A new and complete science-based program for overcoming reading problems at any level*. New York: Knopf.

Shure, M. B. (1992). *I can problem solve: Intermediate elementary grades*. Champaign, IL: Research Press.

Shure, M. B., with Digeronimo, T. F. (1996). *Raising a thinking child workbook*. New York: Simon & Schuster.

Silver, L. (1992). *The misunderstood child: Guide for parents of children with learning disabilities*. New York: McGraw Hill.

Simmons, R. (2002). *Odd girl out: The hidden culture of aggression in girls*. New York: Harcourt.

Smith, S. (1995). *No easy answers: The learning disabled child at home and at school*. New York: Bantam Books.

Solden, S. (1995). *Women with Attention Deficit Disorder*. Nevada City, CA: Underwood Books.

Specter, C. C. (1997). *Saying one thing, meaning another: Activities for clarifying ambiguous language*. Austin: TX: Thinking Publications.

Stevens, S. H. (1999). *The LD child and the ADHD child: Ways parents and professionals can help.* Winston-Salem, NC: Blair.

Swanson, H. L., Hoskyn, M., & Lee, C. (1999). *Interventions for students with learning disabilities: A meta-analysis of treatment outcomes.* New York: Guilford Press.

Tannen, D. (1992). *You just don't understand: Women and men in conversation.* New York: Ballantine Books.

Thompson, M. (2001). *Best friends, worst enemies.* New York: Ballantine Books.

Thompson, S. (1997). *The source for nonverbal learning disorders.* Moline, IL: LinguiSystem.

Ultimate Learning. *Ultimate Learning fun with feelings, Version 1.0.* Available as download at http://www.ultimatelearning.net/products/funwithfeelings.html.

Walker, H. M., McConnell, S., Holmes, D., Todis, B., Walker, J. & Golden, N. (1983). *The Walker Social skills curriculum: The ACCEPTS Program.* Austin, TX: Pro-Ed.

Walker, H. M., Colvin, G., & Ramsey, E. (1995). *Antisocial behavior in school: Strategies and best practices.* Pacific Grove, CA: Brooks/Cole.

Watzlawick, P., Breavin, J., & Jackson, D. D. (1967). *The pragmatics of human communication.* New York: Norton.

Whalen, C., & Schreibman, L. (2003). Joint attention training for children with autism using behavior modification procedures. *Journal of Child Psychology and Psychiatry, 44,* 456–468.

Whitham, C. (1991). *Win the whining war and other skirmishes: A family peace plan.* Los Angeles: Perspective.

Winner, M. G. (2009). *Thinking about you thinking about me.* San Jose, CA: Think Social.

Winner, M. G., & Crooke, P. (2009). *Socially curious and curiously social: A social thinking guidebook for teens and young adults with Asperger's, ADHD, PDD-NOS, NVLD, or other murky undiagnosed social learning issues.* San Jose, CA: Think Social.

Wiseman, R. (2002). *Queen bees and wannabes: Helping your daughter survive cliques, gossip, boyfriends, and other realities of adolescence.* New York: Random House.

Web Sites

Asperger's Syndrome

AspergerPlanet (www.AspergerPlanet.com). The Web site of teacher Maureen Donehey; has an active listserv and is also available in Spanish.

Asperger's Syndrome Education Network (www.ASPEN.com). A national nonprofit organization that provides education and support to families and individuals; holds biyearly conferences.

Autism Society of America (www.autism-society.org). Hosts a national conference and has local state chapters. It is a good resource.

Janet Z. Giler, PhD (www.addept.org). Lots of information on parenting, study skills, behavior management, what therapists need to know, and so on.

Global and Regional Asperger Syndrome Partnership, Inc. (www.grasp.org). New York–based group for adults with Asperger's and their parents and family.

Interactive Autism Network (IAN) (www.iancommunity.org). Sponsored by the Kennedy Kreiger Institute in Washington, DC.

Online Asperger's Syndrome Information and Support (OASIS) (www.udel.edu/bkirby/asperger). A collection of various resources on AS.

WrongPlanet (www.WrongPlanet.com). A Web community designed for individuals with Asperger's Syndrome.

Yale University Child Study Center (http://medicine.yale.edu/childstudy/autism).

Assistive Technology

DotoLearn (www.Dotolearn.com). A great site with information and resources for parents, including visual teaching aids—for example, visual schedules with step-by-step pictures; and reminder strips, visual pictures of the steps to be done for a specific task.

IntelliTools (www.IntelliTools.com). Technology adaptations for children with learning disabilities.

Attention Deficit Hyperactivity Disorder

Attention Deficit Hyperactivity Disorder International Society (www.addis.co.uk/ADDISS). Based in London, a nonprofit organization that holds annual conferences and European support groups.

Janet Z. Giler, PhD (www.addept.org). Lots of information on parenting, study skills, behavior management, what therapists need to know, and so on.

Sam Goldstein, PhD (www.samgoldstein.com). A wonderful Web site by psychologist and educator Dr. Goldstein.

International Association for Children and Adults with Attention Deficit Hyperactivity Disorder (www.chadd.org). Holds international conference every year, and has regional chapters in many large cities throughout the United States.

National Institutes of Health (www.nih.gov). U.S. government site that posts a position paper on ADHD as well as the results of many ongoing studies on ADHD, the role of genetics, mediation, longitudinal studies, effects on girls, and so on.

Learning Disabilities

Biofeedback Certification Institute of America (www.aapb.org). The national cite for certified practitioners of biofeedback and neurofeedback.

Dyslexia Awareness and Resource Center (www.dyslexia-center.com). A Santa Barbara–based support center for parents with children with all forms of learning disabilities; holds an annual conference and is involved in parent advocacy; maintains a huge lending library (reading curriculums, DVDs, books, audiotapes).

GreatSchools (www.greatschools.org). Originally started by www.schwablearning.org that now functions to honor schools and teachers who have successful programs for all disabled children. Also includes current topics.

Learning Disabilities Association of America (www.lda.org). National organization that supports parents and educators with current information about learning disabilities; holds an annual conference, and there are local, state, and regional chapters.

Learning Disabilities Association of California (www.ldaca.org). Holds an annual conference. Maintains a bookstore and resource list for people in California.

Learning Disabilities Resources (www.ldresources.com). An excellent site that contains extensive resources and links for the learning disabilities community and the use of technology.

National Council for Exceptional Children (www.cecsped.org). A federally sponsored clearinghouse on all special needs; has local chapters; holds an annual conference.

Team of Advocates for Special Kids (TASK) (www.taskca.org). Federally Funded nonprofit to connect parents with information and training; informs parents of their legal rights under IDEA; state organizations usually hold trainings.

WETA (www.LDonline). WETA sponsors this comprehensive clearinghouse site.

Books, Technology, and Therapy

ADD Warehouse (www.addwarehouse.com). Sells books and other resources geared toward the ADHD population.

ADDvance (www.addvance.com). Web site and magazine for women with ADHD.

Autism Asperger Publishing (http://www.asperger.net). Comprehensive site with a large selection of books relating to autism and Asperger's Syndrome.

Autism Movement Therapy (www.AutismMovementTherapy.com). An approach to the coordination issues for children in the ASD spectrum, with a funny section on learning break dancing.

Don Johnston (www.donjohnston.com). Specializes in remedial writing programs for younger children.

Feldenkrais Guild of North America (www.feldenkrais.com). Another method of working with sensory deficits; designed by Moshe Feldenkrais.

Franklin Learning Resources (www.franklin.com). Offers electronic aids for learning, such as spelling checkers and translators.

Jessica Kingsley Publisher (www.jkp.com). Publisher of many books on ASD.

Model Me Kids (www.modelmekids.com). This is a for-profit site. The organization has created a number of DVDs to show children how to do specific social skills. Half of my clients found them very useful.

Recording for the Blind and Dyslexic (www.rfbd.org). The largest collection of audiobooks available. This organization provides audio textbooks to any qualifying disabled student for a minor membership fee.

Sensory Integration International (no Web site at this time). 1602 Cabrillo Ave., Torrance, CA 90501-2819. Phone: (310) 320-9986. Jean Ayers created this group and defined her own methodology to help children with sensory processing deficits. This work is often done by occupational therapists or certified practitioners.

Special Needs Project (www.specialneedsproject.com). Has a huge inventory of books on special needs.

Index

IQ tests, 188, 189
IVA computerized test, 185
Izzo, I. D., 22, 146

J

Jacklin, C. N., 141
Jackson, D. D., 3, 160
Jahromi, L. B., 23
Jetton, J., 142, 146
Johnston, C., 48
Joint attention, 17; and Asperger's Syndrome, 191; parent and child sharing, 17; teacher and student sharing, 20; teaching, 16
Joint perception, 9; and acquisition deficits, 19; how self-evaluation forms can be used to create, 37–38; and structured feedback, 33
Joking, 35; and difficulty recognizing and labeling feelings, 10; and rules for telling jokes, 156–158

K

Kaiser, N. M., 48
Kasari, C., 16, 22–23, 191
Kehr, J., 1
Kennedy, D. N., 189
Kids Online (PBS), 178
Kinesis, 13
Klein, R. G., 22
Koegel, L., 23
Koegel, R., 23
Konig, P. H., 22
Kraus, I., 142, 146

L

Lande, A., 53
Language difficulties: and hidden rules of conversation, 9–10; and joint attention, 16; special problems due to, 9
Lara, J., 53
Last One Picked, First One Picked On (video; Lavoie), 1
Latency years, 13
Laugeson, E. A., 22, 146
Lavoie, R., 1, 25
Learning disabilities, 48; comorbidity of ADHD with, 184; evaluation for, 188–189; identifying, 187–188; possible school-based services for, 188; resources for, 201
Learning Experiences: Alternative Program for Preschoolers, 23
Listening, 35; active, 77, 91; and adding to story, 97; and asking questions, 78–79; and being good listener, 21, 74–86; and being poor listener, 76; body language of, 76–77; eye contact exercise for, 84–85; facts (exercise), 83; mistakes, 75–76; overview of, 74–75; and perseveration, 79–81; and responding, 77; and right way to listen, 77; and Self-Evaluation Form: Listening, 41; two parts of, 75. *See also* Conversational skills
Loftus, R., 22
Lord, C., 16, 22–23
Los Angeles, California, 1

M

Maccoby, E. E., 141, 142
Maedgen, J. W., 23
Manis, F., 189
Mannerisms, repetitive, 193
Manners, teaching, 52–53. *See also* Etiquette
Mannuzza, S., 22
McGinnis, E., 55
Medication: for performance problems, 18; trials, for ADHD, 185
Mellon, D., 3, 14
Memory, 189, 1365
Meta-comminication, 3; and joint perception, 19; meaning of, 4; and mind-blindness, 9
Meta-message, 102; and cell phone use, 175
Mick, E., 142, 146
Mimicking, 12, 114; and acquisition deficits, 19; gestures and tones of others to appear "in sync," 102, 114; resource for, 122
Mind reading, 3, 4, 9, 33; disapproval, 21
Mind Reading: An Interactive Guide to Emotion (Baron-Cohen), 122
Mind-blindness, 4; how, causes conflicts, 11; and teaching social skills, 8–9
Mirroring, 105, 115
Mitchell, P., 191
Monotone, speaking in, 116, 193
Mood regulation, and girls friendships, 142
Moodiness, and ADHD, 183
Mosovich, S., 193
Mt. Sinai Medical Center, 193
Mundy, P., 16, 19, 23, 191
Musical training, 50; and musical concepts that use good social skills, 115; to teach emotional harmony, 114–115
My Turn, Your Turn: Songs for Building Social Skills, 122
Myatt, R., 11
Myles, B. S., 168–169
MySpace, 143, 176, 177

N

National Joint Committee on Learning Disabilities, 188
Neuroplasticity, 16
"News of difference," 31
Nintendo Wii, 53
NLD. *See* Nonverbal Learning Disability
Nolt, C., 1
Nonverbal communication: body checklist for, 104; and nonverbal messages, 35; signals and gestures in, 102; skills in, 35. *See also* Body language
Nonverbal Learning Disability (NLD), 1, 11, 19, 122, 187, 188, 193; and "positive illusory bias," 48; possible school-based services for, 188; and understanding tone, 113, 116
Novotny, S., 193

O

Obsessive routines, and Asperger's Syndrome, 192
Ohan, J. L., 48
Omissions, correcting, 40
1,2,3, Magic (Phelan), 40
Opportunistic reinforcement, 31–32, 38